RECOVERY TODAY

The Shepherd's way

Volume 1

KANDI ROSE MINISTRIES
Perryville, Arkansas

Copyright   2011
KANDI ROSE

All rights reserved. No reproduction of this book in any form, such as electronic, mechanical, photocopying, recording or storing in a retrieval system etc. without permission. That permission must be in writing by the author or publisher.

ISBN: 978-0-9766197-5-8

First Printing   Feb. 2011
Second Printing   Oct. 2011

To purchase additional copies of, "RECOVERY TODAY", volume One, or to contact the author, Evangelist Kandi Rose, log on:

www.kandiroseministries.com

Kandi is also the author of her autobiography, "Spirits of Seduction/Free at Last". Also Recovery Today Volume 2 is available for purchase. .If you would like a copy of any of these books, log on to her website. Please specify which books you would like. God Bless!

Evangelist Kandi Rose hosts her own TV program, "Addiction Free," and can be watched on her Youtube channel.

Kandi Rose is not only an Author / TV Host but also an Evangelist. To invite her to minister, visit her website.

**Edited by Rev. Mark Haston,
Senior Pastor of Hot Springs First Assembly of God
(except the testimony section)**

Recovery Today
12 Truths to Freedom

1. Ps. 51:3
Acknowledge our sin & we cannot change our self

2. Jn. 1:12
Believe and apply God's written word

3. Rms. 10:9-10
Commit our life to God through Jesus Christ

4. Ps. 51:6
Examine destructive actions and inward attitudes

5. Gal. 6:2
Share with others what has happened in our life

6. Ps.51:17
Be willing to **Turn** from a lifestyle of sin

7. 1 Jn. 1:9
With humility we ask Jesus Christ to **Change** us.

8. Mt. 5:23-24
Reconcile with those we hurt in the past or present

9. Eph. 4:31-32
Stop **Blaming** and forgive those who have hurt us

10. Lam. 3:40
Daily examine our self and ask God's forgiveness

11. Col. 1:9-10
Have a **Personal Relationship** with him, seeking his will

12. Mt. 28:19-20
Living a Godly lifestyle, we **Help Others Recover**

> **Isa. 53: 6**
> All we like sheep have gone astray; we have turned every one to his own way; and the Lord hath laid on him the iniquity of us all.
>
> **Luke 19: 10**
> The Good Shepherd has come to Seek & Save that which is lost.
>
> He died to Recover all mankind. It is our choice to allow him to rescue us.

Definition of **LOSE:**
Bring to destruction; to suffer loss or separation from; fail to keep control of; fail to use; let slip; fail to win, gain or obtain; undergo defeat; fail to keep, maintain or sustain; to wander or go astray from; fail to advance or improve.

Definition of **LOST:**
Not made use of, won or claimed; unable to find the way; ruined or destroyed physically or morally; no longer known; taken away or beyond reach; hardened; insensible.

Definition of **FIND**:
To come upon by searching; effort to gain or regain the use or power of; a valuable item of discovery

Definition of **RECOVER:**
To get back to normal position or condition; rescue, to reclaim; obtain a final legal judgment in one's favor; to recover again or renew.

MISSION & PURPOSE

The book, "Recovery Today", has 3 purposes in 1. One of those purposes is as a *Recovery* book to help people with any kind of habit or addiction. *New Christians* this book is to assist you in *discipleship.* Christians you will find this as *a great tool for evangelism*

These life lessons through the empowering of the Holy Spirit, using God's written Word, will enable us all to understand *why* we must be saved but also *how* to be saved and then how to *spiritually grow* to be more like him. Then we can use these life lessons to *disciple others, becoming a mentor.*

Any addiction, habit, attitude, or sin of any kind will be broken as truth is revealed to His hurting people. Jesus tells us in John 8:32, "and ye shall know the truth and the truth shall make you free".

- Truth (if acted upon) empowers us to be free from any addiction or sin.
- Truth (if acted upon) enables us to have a pure relationship with a Holy God through Jesus Christ.

God's written word, the Bible, tells us in Hosea 4:6 "My people are destroyed for lack of knowledge". Truth is found in reading, hearing, and studying the Word of God. In it we find a loving, forgiving, merciful, and powerful God who desires to have a personal relationship with each one of us, His creation.

This book is based on the scriptures, our road map for daily living. These life lessons have been written to enable you to see you can have, *Recovery Today and everyday*, not by your power, but through His.

The mission and purpose of this book is to guide countless millions of hurting people to the one who loves them and died for them, Jesus Christ. He is the only one who has all power, and who wants to give his power to us so that we can live a victorious life.

These lessons are even for those who've never had any habits or addiction, but desire to be more like Jesus! This study will help your character, enabling you to be a better witness to all those in your life. This is definitely for those who now not only have a relationship with The Good Shepherd and living free from sin, but desiring to be used by God.

Since these 12 truths are based upon God's written word, the Bible, I believe we all can benefit by becoming more like Jesus! This workbook has life lessons that are based on the Holy Scriptures. They were written so that anyone with any type of addiction or sin would be able to relate their own personal life situations to them. People who have never had an addiction will benefit.

The Word of God tells us we all have been born with a sinful nature, so everyone will be able to relate in some way. *After going through these lessons you will be better equipped to help others!* If you have been in any kind of addiction and been set free, your life can be a great inspiration to others of what God can do. You just might be the messenger God wants to use!

In what ways can this book be used to help people?

This book has life lessons that can be utilized in several ways:
- On an individual basis
- One on one, learning with a mentor, friend, family, etc.
- As a Bible Study group with someone leading in a home, church, or some other facility
- Used strictly as a Recovery group
- Utilized as a discipleship study
- As a Soul winners, Evangelism class
- Or use as a 3 in 1 group, encompassing all purposes

SPECIAL NOTE

In this study guide, there is a reference section at the conclusion of each lesson. It is included for those who do not have a Bible available to refer to when studying. Scriptures are printed from the King James Version.

True Stories of RECOVERY

Table of Contents

1. **Spirits of Seduction**/Free at Last
   By Author/TV Host
   Evangelist Kandi Rose

2. **How to Beat The Odds**/The Gambler
   By Author/TV & Radio Host
   Tommy Thomas

3. Bitter & Angry-**She Surrendered All**
   By Judy

4. **Meth Brings Misery**
   God brings Deliverance
   By Tammy

"Spirits of Seduction"
Free at Last
Autobiography of Kandi Rose

The author of this book was a former Stripper & Prostitute, who had **Multiple Addictions**, once owning her own Strip-O-Gram business in the Chicago area.

Is Prayer Important? Does God hear and Answer Prayers? Does our Actions & Attitudes affect others lives? Is there a Spiritual battle between Good and Evil that influences Our Choices? Do our Choices have Consequences? Can Our Choices affect Our Destiny?

I, Kandi Rose, know firsthand the answer to the entire above Yes! Yes! Yes! First of all I want to thank My Lord and Savior, Jesus Christ, for rescuing me. I was lost but now I'm found. Now if you'd ask me years ago if I was lost, I'd said you were crazy. Actually at the time I felt that I was a very successful businesswoman doing what I loved, dancing. You see prior to meeting my Good Shepherd Jesus, I owned my own *Strip-O-Gram business called, "Kandi Rose Productions.* I had 26 people working for me. I had not only male and female strippers, including myself but acquired other talented people that I choreographed for variety shows in nightclubs. I advertised on billboard, commercial on Cable TV, 5 radio stations, yellow pages, newspapers and made personal appearances at festivals and fairs signing autographs.

I'd like to take you back to my childhood and tell you how I ended up in such an X-Rated lifestyle.

The first chapter of my book is called, *Daddy's Demons*. My father appeared to all as such a wonderful husband and father. I was an only child and really loved my daddy until I realized he was perpetrating evil acts on me. My mother had no idea, as he was very cunning and sneaky. After years of this sexual and emotional torment, I couldn't take it anymore and let this dark secret out. My mom is such a kind and loving woman and she and I were very close. I am so grateful she believed me and at that time of my life lying was not part of my character. Soon after that with suitcases in hand, no car, we hopped on the bus and moved to another neighborhood in Chicago, renting a 3-room apartment. Bitterness and hatred came to reside in our hearts for years as more heartaches and disappointments piled on.

Mom grieved and fell into depression. I started hanging with the street kids in the neighborhood and my innocence soon became a victim of prey for more evil that awaited me. In chapter 2 of my book reveals that our choices do have consequences. Since I began to look for love and acceptance like most young people and adults do, in all the wrong places and faces, I became a victim of *date rape, gang rape and was even kidnapped at 5 months pregnant at knife point.* At 16 I acquired a false I.D. and hung out in bars and nightclubs. This started a life of multiple addictions, alcohol, drugs, gambling, pornography and many other evils soon evolved in a very X-Rated lifestyle. At 18 I was introduced to an agent that booked me into 33 nightclubs in the Chicago land area and even in Indiana as a go-go dancer. Many of the clubs I worked in were the Rush Street and Old Town areas.

These bad choices led to many heartaches and horrible consequences.

At age 18 I became pregnant with my oldest daughter. Her father went to jail 3 days before she was born. A month after she was born I met a drummer and had a boy and girl by him within 2 and a half year time. He was a womanizer; and even cheated with my best friend. Soon after that heartbreaking episode I met a man just home from Viet Nam. I was quite impressed as he had a good job, all the others were dead beats; brand new car and he liked all 3 of the kids. I was infatuated but not in love. I saw this as security for myself and the kids, a real family situation. After a year living together this would be my first marriage relationship. He adopted all 3 kids and we even had a daughter together. We bought a brand new house in the suburbs of

Chicago. Instead of a happy home, years of addictions and unhealed brokenness from childhood, caused it to be wrecked.

Chapter 6 of my book is titled, *Divorced and Desperate*. After 10 years of marriage that ended up with domestic violence, I resorted back to what I knew would give me lots of money, dancing. I answered an ad in the paper for a Strip Club. This would be an even more degrading job. The night would start off dressed in beautiful elaborate costumes and end up fully nude at the end. The worst was hustling the men in a darkened room to spend all their money and max out their charge cards. I stayed high all the time and my heart got so hardened. After a year of that I quit. My boyfriend at that time had a friend who was having a bachelor party. He offered to pay me 150.00 for a half hour if I would come with my costumes and music and end up doing a full strip for the last few minutes. I thought this was so awesome, as my boyfriend would be my bodyguard and no one would physically touch me. I'd just entertain so to speak. As I mentioned previously I turned this into a full-blown business and with much advertising was well on my way to potential riches.

Praise God, the Lord does answer parent's prayers!

A few years earlier my mom had got born again and married a wonderful man who also became a Christian. They were such an *influence* in my life. They not only *talked the talk* but they *walked the walk*. One night I received a phone call and I thought my children were going to have to go to a foster home. Well this was more than I could bear. I needed peace to deal with this and my mind went to my mom who always had peace and joy no matter what she went through. For years she suffered with such physical torment of osteoporosis, fibromyalgia and rheumatoid arthritis. Her attitude was amazing through it all. My step-dad, who is an awesome dad, is an amazing man of God who always showed acts of kindness even though I had such an evil lifestyle. Unconditional Love was extended to me that ultimately showed me God's love. Now I realize what had transpired. My precious Savior was wooing me by His Holy Spirit and telling me to reflect on my parent's lives. He showed me that, he made the difference in their lives and he wanted to do the same for me. Wow! What love! I called my mom and she ended up, spiritually birthing me into the kingdom through a prayer of repentance. Chapter 7 of my book is called, "The Choice that Affected my Destiny".

For those who have backslid I have a confession

NOTE: That testimony is about my life only up to age 35 when I met the love of my life, Jesus. For three and one-half years I did not just talk the talk, I walked it. Unfortunately I let the spirit of loneliness overtake me. For the record, no man or woman is worth losing your soul and ruining your relationship with the Lord. That is what I let happen though my own choice. I met a man and ended up sleeping with him only to return to most of my sinful ways for two miserable wasted years. God kept tugging on my heart and sent so many messages and messengers my way that I surrendered to the Lord. I am more determined now than ever to stay on the path of holiness and take as many people with me to heaven by my testimony.

After having no peace and no more purpose in life, I finally listened once again to the voice of love calling me to return to my first love. Life had become miserable again and I missed that pure clean relationship I had once enjoyed with the love of my life, Jesus. At this time I have been, Freed by the Truth once again for almost 22 years. There's been total abstinence from all addictions. God has taken out the hard heart of hatred and has given me a soft loving heart with a definite attitude adjustment. I am not bragging on myself because self did not change me; God did. Of course I'm not perfect and my character is still being, a work in progress. I am not in intentional sin though as years past. My heart's desire is to tell, Recovery is possible only through,

The Shepherd's Way!

How To Beat The Odds
The Gambler
By Tommy Thomas

It was an exceptionally warm spring day in 1974. The sun was bright but you couldn't tell because of the old, stained curtains covering the nursing home windows. I was playing cards with my 82-year-old father, *Titanic Thompson*. He was one of the *most famous gamblers and golfers in the world.*

Before I walked out of the nursing home that spring day, my dad did something he hadn't done before. He put his arms around me and said, "I love you son." I had waited my whole life to hear those words. Little did I realize as I walked out of his room that day, I would never see my dad again. He died just a few days later.

My dad had divorced my mother when I was 2 years old. I grew up reading about him in Life magazine, Golf Digest and Sports Illustrated. I wanted him to love me and felt the best way to do that was to become a professional gambler. I started practicing with a deck of cards when I was 13. The best card cheaters in the world would come to see dad, and I would spend hours mastering what they taught me.

Dad told me I was the best he had ever seen with a deck of cards, but he never told me he loved me.

In 1997, four weeks before Easter, I took a look at myself in the mirror and didn't like what I saw. I said, "God, I have been taking from people all my life. When I die, I want someone to remember me for giving instead of taking." I fell down on my knees and cried out to Him.

Two weeks later, I was waiting for my turn in a barbershop when I met a Christian lady named Margaret Moberly. Even though we had never met before, she knew everything about me.

She said that God had told her, "That man is a professional gambler. He has a lot of nice things, but he isn't happy. He has a big heart, and God has him on a long leash." I was blown away.

I responded, "Lady, it doesn't get any better than being on a long leash with God, does it?" She didn't laugh. The night before Easter she sent me another message through a friend, "tell him that God now has him on a short leash, *the devil has made a bet on his soul, and God has covered the bet."* God had really gotten my attention now.

That Easter I went to church with Margaret. Again, prompted by the Lord, she said, "Tommy, when you were a teen-ager, God called you to be an evangelist and everything in your life has led up to that end." When she said those words, I felt like someone poured hot oil in me. I have never been the same since.

I knew then there would only be two winning hands, and they were nailed to the cross for me.

I am now *a volunteer chaplain* and have preached the gospel in maximum-security prisons for the last five years. I am so thankful that God never gave up on me. He has given me the love that I was looking for and given me a new purpose in life. I know that God loves me, not because of my ability or performance, but because He is my Father, and I am His kid.

NOTE: Tommy Thomas had his own TV program, which aired weekly on Angel One Network, called, How to beat the Odds. He interviewed folks who have been set free from all kinds of habits, attitudes & addictions. I, Kandi Rose was aired on his program Sept. 2007. He has also written a book called, "God & The Gambler". He now has a radio program.

Log on to his website: www.howtobeattheodds.com
© 2002-2008

She SURRENDERED All
By Judy

On February 4 1994 I took my last drink and drug. I came to the saving grace of my Lord Jesus Christ! That was the day I accepted Jesus into my life and started my journey of recovery.

Before that day my life was a mess!

I was the sixth child born to a family of ten children and my family was drinkers and addicts. My family came from a generation of organized criminals with a very sinful nature. I was getting molested at a very early age from different family members for a few years. I was not alone in this for I do think that *almost all of us kids were molested at some time* in our childhood. We were either getting verbally, emotionally, physically or sexually abuse each and every day. There were fights in our house pretty much on a daily schedule, and when the police were called, they dreaded having to deal with my Dad. Only the State Police or higher ups would arrest my Dad for the local police were afraid of him and with good reason.

There was so much hate and shame in our family I hated living and always thought death would be better than the life I was leading. I was a very sad, angry, and scared little girl. I grew up thinking that there was no God for if he was real, then where was he when I needed him! We were forced to go to church as children, but the only way God's name was ever used in our house was in vain. I learned early that the best way to stay out of harm's way was to be out of the house as much as possible.

I started working at the age of ten, but I had to give the money to Mom. That was a big deal for me, for I did not have to be around all of the craziness that went on. I became very involved in sports and reading and was a good student.

When I was eighteen, I married a guy just like my Dad!

Go figure!

That only lasted for two years, as he cheated on me and beat me just like Dad! However, I was such an angry person that I fought back with great rage. We had a terrible marriage and when I got divorced at twenty, I started drinking and drugging with a sexual sinful nature. I was in college and made good grades but was out of control!

I got married again at twenty-three and I am still married to that husband. We had good times and bad times, but we partied on and off until the end of my drinking. I drank daily and if I was awake I was drinking or drugging. I was very messed up in my thinking and Satan had a foothold in my life. I had sexual sin in my life and was hooked on any sexual high I could get. I was a very angry woman and learned martial arts just to misuse it, when I could. If I could hit a man it made me feel like I was getting even for the wrong that had been done to me. So this craziness went on for twenty years!

We had two children and became a bad example for our kids.

However, glad to say we never beat or molested them. I'm sorry to say though they witnessed our drunken behavior. They also were exposed to my physical abuse to our men friends when I felt they needed a beating for whatever reason I decided on!

Then one day a friend invited me to go to church and I didn't think I really wanted to as *I was planning on killing myself* that day. I thought, what did I have to lose by trying it? I went and it was kind of nice, but I still did not trust that there was a God! I kept going back to church and I was starting to change the way I was thinking, but I was not going to give up the drinking and drugging for it killed the pain that was inside my soul. Then one day I went and they were singing, *"I Surrender All"*, and I knew that was what I had to do! I went to the altar call and surrendered all to my Lord Jesus whom I knew was alive forever more. That was the day I put the drinking and drugging down for the very last time! I started a program of recovery and I have been clean and free for over fourteen years.

I have seen so many miracles of the Lord in my life and others! One of the greatest was that I forgave my Dad and other members of my family and led them to the Lord. Before my Dad died he was a child of God and led others to the Lord. I realized that through Christ all things are possible.

Today, I have a great life, marriage and relationship with my family and others. I live my life for Jesus, for he is the driving force in my life and he keeps me safe, happy and free of the past that used to haunt me and kept me in a world of darkness. I encourage everyone, no matter what has ever happened in your life to turn to him, confess your sin, turn from your sin and follow Jesus.

He will bring you out of darkness and you can live a sober life in him!

I also want to say that God put Kandi in my life to teach me his ways and I will forever be thankful for the love of Jesus she has always shown me. I love you so much! Thanks for all you do for God's kingdom Kandi!
Love, Judy

Note from Kandi, the author:

Judy is a committed Christian who loves the Lord, not with just lip service but walks the walk. I met her years ago. God puts good Christian friends in our life to not only help each other but to reach others for Him. She is one of my best friends. We dressed as an angel and devil. We went to countless alcohol, drug treatment centers doing drama and telling about our Higher Power Jesus Christ. What a high! What a joy that was!

Judy now mentors several women who have been wounded in their lives. She points them to Jesus, who is the only one who can heal all of our broken hearts and make us have *Recovery Today and Everyday!*

Psalm 147:3   He healeth the *broken in heart* and bindeth up their wounds. *Surrender all* and *let God use your life*!

METH Brings MISERY
By Tammy

GOD Brings DELIVERANCE

I don't really know where to start really. I thought a lot about my testimony. I guess I just never realized how hard it would be to put it into words, but here goes. The misery all started in the early 90's when my husband and I started using meth. In the beginning we only used on weekends. My husband was dedicated to his job and I was a housewife who loved nothing more than taking care of my husband and our three beautiful daughters. It seemed we kept things under control for a while but as time went on we were using more and more.

After a couple of years we met some people who were meth cooks. My husband wanted to learn how to cook, and that's exactly what he did. At the time we thought it was the greatest thing. We could have all we wanted, whenever we wanted it. I remember thinking what a great drug it was. I could lose weight and keep my house spotless. My husband was a partner in an up and coming concrete business but about 6 months after being a cook, he just walked away from the business. Shortly after he was arrested for possession and placed on probation. This didn't slow us down though. I can remember talking to his probation officer. He told us meth tears apart families and we thought, not ours. I guess I'll never forget that conversation.

We spent the next couple of years moving around here and there trying to get one step ahead of the police. Our daughters were getting further and further behind in school. Our two youngest, they're twins, had already failed kindergarten and first grade. In 1998 my husband and some of his friends were cooking in a very public place when someone smelled the odor and called 911.

The police came and found the lab.

Everyone was arrested but by the grace of God, my husband was able to get past them. He ran into the woods and spent the night by some railroad tracks. By the time he got to us the next day he was as white as a ghost, freezing and scared to death. One of his friends gave the police his name and we heard wanted posters had been put out. So we went on the run for a few days until things cooled down. We went to another county and stayed with some friends

Thirteen days later my husband and I had a special night just for the two of us. He wanted to cook a batch first so we could have money and dope so I waited at a relatives' house. While I was waiting someone came and told me to get to the hospital because my husband had been severely burned. By the time I got to the E.R. they were already putting him into an ambulance to transfer him to the burn unit at Children's Hospital. He was all wrapped up and black and blue. The first 24 hours were miserable. I guess he thought he was still on fire because he just kept fighting and kicking. They weren't able to give him anything for pain because of all the drugs he already had in his system.

He was burned on both of his arms, chest and neck.

After several skin graphs and a lot of pain, he was released from the hospital. We didn't have a house of our own to go to, so we went to his sister's to recover. All during his recovery we decided that we were through with this monster of misery that was taking everything from us. As we starting wanting our own place again, we realized cooking was a quick way to make money to do it. It wasn't long until we were living in a nice house. I was driving a nice car and we could afford anything we wanted. Things were as good as it gets for a while.

Then in the year 2000 I found out that my friend that was staying with us was also my husband's girlfriend. I was devastated. Soon after that he moved out. I was on my own for the first time with no money and 3 daughters to take care of. I couldn't even take care of myself, as I had no job skills with no clue as to what to do. I did have one true friend and I thank God for her because she taught me how to make a meal out of Mac & cheese and peanut butter. It wasn't long until the utilities were shut off and then came the eviction notice. By this time my sister-in-law had moved out of her house and agreed to let us move in if my husband paid the utilities. It wasn't long until the electricity was turned off there as well. In the meantime my drug habit was suffering though I had plenty of friends keeping me supplied.

We wound up in a battered woman's shelter until we could be placed in government housing.

Shortly after I got my first possession of meth charge and was evicted again. Thank God my mom and sister took my girls, got them in church and school, giving them stability. I stayed here and there; sometimes I would go stay with my mom and girls and go to church. My addiction would take control and off I'd go again. I would leave while the girls were in bed or at school. I kept on hurting them over and over again. I finally moved back home with my family, even went to church but I continued to use meth, just not as often.

Now I've been clean for 15 months. I even quit smoking cigarettes 11 months ago. Praise God! My oldest daughter is married now and I have a beautiful 7-month-old granddaughter. I believe God gave me a second chance with her. My other daughters and I attend church together every Sunday and our lives are totally different. I'm so blessed that I had a family that never stopped praying for me, and a merciful God that thought I was worth saving. As I look back it's apparent to me now that through all this God was right there with us the whole time. Even in the midst of all our sin, He was right there, watching over us, carrying us when we couldn't stand alone. I'm thankful that I serve a God who is able to deliver me from my addictions and set me free. I have:

Recovery Today and Everyday!

TABLE OF CONTENTS
12   Life Lessons

1   Acknowledge or Deny

2   Believe and Receive

3   Self-Will or God's Will

4   X-treme Character Makeover

5   Sharing - The Healing Begins

6   Rebellion or Submission

7   Change or Same ole-Same ole

8   I'm Sorry brings Peace

9   Same Blame Game

10   L.U.I. Living Under the Influence

11   Intimacy with My Shepherd

12   Purpose – Help others Recover

Acknowledge or Deny

Lesson 1
Ps. 51:3
ACKNOWLEDGE our sin & we cannot change our self

A. Write Psalm 51:3 (Please read aloud)

_____
_____

Definition of **ACKNOWLEDGE:**
Accept, admit, own up to, recognize, concede, yield, take notice of, confess / agree to the idea of declaring something to be true; something previously denied or doubted; an admission of wrong doing and shortcoming

The opposite of acknowledge:
Reject, renounce, deny, ignore, disregard

B. What keeps us from acknowledging or admitting to anything that's negative? _____

C. Write: Pro. 16:18 (Please read aloud)

_____
_____

D. Proverbs 29:23 (Please read aloud)

_____
_____

Definition of **ADDICT:**
To devote or surrender oneself to something habitually or obsessively

Definition of **HABIT:**
Practice, usage, way of acting through repetition, unconsciously

and often compulsively, practice suggests an act or method often followed regularly, through choice

Definition of **SIN**:
Offense against God, transgression, iniquity, falling stray, doing any wrong, evil, ungodly or immoral act

The Greek and Hebrew meaning of sin means "missing the mark", like a misguided arrow shot at a target. We miss God's plan for our lives when we don't allow him to guide us. Addiction and sin causes us to miss the target. The arrow representing our lives without God's guidance is a life that strays off and becomes lost.

Definition of **INIQUITY:**
Wickedness, wrongdoing, evil doing, sin, transgression, abomination, sinfulness, immorality

Definition of **TRANSGRESSION:**
Offense, sin, trespass, wrongdoing, law breaking, crime

Definition of **TRESPASS:**
Enter unlawfully, intrude, invade, sin, wrongdoing, immorality, stepping across property lines or other people's personal boundaries

NOTE: We trespass against God when we overstep his guidelines for us that are in his written Word, the Holy Bible.

Definition of **FREEDOM:**
Liberty, no longer in slavery or bondage, not captive anymore

Definition of **BONDAGE:**
Slavery, captivity, held against a person's will

E. The Bible tells us we are all born with a sinful nature because of Adam and Eve. Write out Genesis 3:6

_____
_____

F. When Adam and Eve didn't obey God; it brought sin into the world. So therefore their children and the whole world's population since then have been born with a sinful nature. We all are born into bondage (slavery to this sinful nature). Read & write out Romans 5:12

_____
_____
_____

G. That is why we need a new nature as we cannot change ourselves and be sin & addiction free without God's help. Read & write Romans 5:17

_____
_____
_____

H. Write down Romans 5:19

_____
_____
_____

I. Read, write and memorize John 3:16   (Please read aloud)

_____
_____

J. How can someone get this new nature and does God require everyone to have it? Is it just for people who have habits and addictions or do seemingly good moral people need it as well? Read, write and memorize John 3:3:

_____
_____

K. Read Romans 7:15-25 and see if you can relate your own character traits to these verses. Do you recognize the sinful nature in your own past and present life? Are there areas in your own life you've tried to change and couldn't? Do you feel you've been a slave to certain choices and behaviors you've made? Write your thoughts down.

_____
_____
_____

L. What are some of the habits and attitudes that have caused you to suffer?

_____
_____
_____

M. Just who are sinners? There are people in this world who don't go to church, but are not criminals and have never been addicted to anything. They are considered good, moral people. Does God view them any differently from those who have led immoral lives? No! Not at all! Here's what God's Word, the Bible, has to say about this. Read and write out Romans 3:10:

_____

N. Write down Romans 3:23   (Please read aloud)

_____

O. From reading those verses what conclusion did you come to as who are sinners?

_____

P. Write down Romans 6:23   (Please read aloud)

_____
_____

Q. How can we become righteous & not sinners? Have you heard the term, "saved"? It refers to being saved from the judgment of God or saved from our sins. Read & write out I Timothy 1:15:

_____
_____

R. Read & write out Romans 5:6

S. Read & write out Romans 5:7-10

_____
_____
_____
_____
_____
_____
_____
_____

T. Do you see from all these scriptures that Jesus suffered and died on the cross to save not only you but whosoever would choose to live for him and cause them to become righteous (in right standing with God)? The cross enables us to be free from all sin and addiction! _____

U. How can a person no longer be a sinner and be saved from their sin nature? Write out Romans 10:13 (Please read aloud)

_____
_____

V. Read & write out Romans 10:9-10 (Please read aloud)

_____
_____
_____
_____
_____

W. Read but not write out, Romans 10:1-3. These verses show us that even in Bible times people did not know how to be saved. They didn't even acknowledge or recognize they were a sinner. Can you see from these scriptures that all have sinned and need a Savior, Jesus Christ? Write your thoughts about your own life pertaining to what the Bible refers to as salvation.

_____
_____

_____
_____
_____
_____

Once we acknowledge our sins and addictions and we confess it with our mouth, can we keep sinning and stay in our addictions and sin of any kind? No! We are saved *from* our sins, **not to** *continue* in them. Read all of Romans chapter 6. People think because they believe in Jesus, go to church or said a prayer at one time, that they are saved. Saved from what? If they're still doing what they used to do, they are rejecting what Christ did on the cross. Our actions show that we don't need or want a Savior, Jesus Christ.

Jesus has been revealing His truth to you through this lesson. He wants you to know how to be saved from your sin and addiction. He loves you so much and wants to have a personal relationship with you. God is Holy and cannot have a pure relationship with us if we allow sin to stay in our lives. He made a way for us to be holy as he is holy, through His Son, Jesus Christ. Don't be deceived in thinking because you talk to God, that everything's fine.

God made a way for us to have the power to overcome sin through the death of His Son. He does not take it lightly when we refuse to stop sinning when he's given His only Son's life to enable you and I to not only become "clean & free" but to stay, "clean & free"
.

I, Kandi Rose, the author and founder of this program acknowledged I was a sinner even when I really was not familiar with that word. I pray this lesson pertaining to step one has helped you today. No matter what lifestyle you've been living, it's not good enough to have that pure and clean relationship with a Holy God. To come to God the Father we all must come by the way of the Cross, which was done for us through the death and resurrection of Jesus Christ.

There is only one way. Jesus said in John 14:6, "I am the way, the truth, and the life. No man cometh unto the Father, but by me." If you'd like to be saved right now, it's very simple. Simply admit that you're a sinner and ask Jesus to forgive your sins. He's been waiting for you to ask. He loves you so much and desires a personal relationship with you. Maybe you've done this before but rebelled and went back to sin and addictions again. As long as you have breath to breathe, you can make a U-turn, so ask again! You are precious to him just as our children are precious to us. Don't let the devil lie to you anymore and keep you from the one who loves you and died for you!

I, Kandi, went back to living like I wanted to after 3 and one half years of living for the Lord. I was so miserable and missed my beautiful clean relationship I once had with him. God's Holy Spirit kept tugging at my heart (just as he's doing to you.) Listen to His voice of love calling you. He's reaching out to you right now, teaching you through this Step Lesson.

If you'd like to **ACKNOWLEDGE** your sins and **TURN** from them just say a simple prayer like this:

JESUS, thank you for reaching me through this lesson. I now **ACKNOWLEDGE** my sins and believe that through the power of your Holy Spirit, I will be able to live a Godly lifestyle. Thank you for forgiving me my sins and loving me so much that you died for me. I'm willing to leave my old lifestyle behind and live for you with my whole heart. I love you Jesus!

AMEN

Reference Section for Acknowledge or Deny

A. Psalm 51:3 For I acknowledge my transgressions and my sin is ever before me.
B. Pride-Ego
C. Proverbs 16:18 Pride goeth before destruction, and a haughty spirit before a fall.
D. Proverbs 29:23 A man's pride shall bring him low: but honor shall uphold the humble in spirit.
E. Genesis 3:6 And when the woman saw that the tree was good for food, and that it was pleasant to the eyes, and a tree to be desired to make one wise, she took of the fruit thereof, and did eat, and gave also unto her husband with her; and he did eat.
F. Romans 5:12 Wherefore, as by one man sin entered into the world, and death by sin; and so death passed upon all men, for that all have sinned.
G. Romans 5:17 For if by one man's offense death reigned by one; much more they which receive abundance of grace and the gift of righteousness shall reign in life by one, Jesus Christ
H. Romans 5:19 For as by one man's disobedience (many were made sinners), even so by the obedience of one man shall many be made righteous.
I. Jn 3:16 For God so loved the world, that He gave His only begotten son, that whosoever believeth in Him should not perish, but have everlasting life.
J. Jn 3:3 Jesus answered and said unto him, Verily, verily, I say unto thee, Except a man be born again, he cannot see the kingdom of God.
M. Romans 3:10 As it is written, there is none righteous, no, not one.
N. Romans 3:23 For all have sinned, and come short of the glory of God.
O. Everyone in the world
P. Romans 6:23 For the wages of sin is death; but the gift of God is eternal life through Jesus Christ our Lord.
Q. I Timothy 1:15 There is a faithful saying and worthy of all

acceptation that Christ Jesus came into the world to save sinners; of whom I am Chief.

R. Romans 5:6 For when we were yet without strength, in due time Christ died for the ungodly.

S. Romans 5:7-10 For scarcely for a righteous man will one die; yet peradventure for a good man some would even dare to die. But God commended His love toward us, in that, while we were yet sinners, Christ died for us. Much more then, being now justified by His blood, we shall be saved from wrath through Him. For if, when we were enemies, we were reconciled to God by the death of His Son, much more, being reconciled, we shall be saved by His life.

T. Yes

U. Romans 10:13 For whosoever shall call upon the name of the Lord shall be saved.

V. Romans 10:9-10 That if thou shalt confess with thy mouth the Lord Jesus, and shalt believe in thine heart that God hath raised him from the dead, (thou shalt be saved). For with the heart man believeth unto righteousness; and with the mouth confession is made unto salvation.

Believe & Receive

Lesson 2
John 1:12
<u>**BELIEVE**</u> and apply God's written Word

A. Write down John 1:12   (Please read aloud)
_____
_____
_____

Synonym for **POWER:**
Authority, control, dominion or command; meaning the right to govern or rule or determine

Definition of **AUTHORITY:**
Granting of power for a specific purpose within specified limits

Definition of **CONTROL:**
Stresses the power to direct and restrain

Definition of **DOMINION:**
Sovereign power or sovereign authority

When we believe Jesus died for our sins we receive not only his forgiveness but also receive His Holy Spirit that empowers us to have control over all addiction and sin. How do we receive the Spirit of God? Read John 3:1-21. This passage contains a phrase you might have heard before, "born again".

B. Write down John 3:3 (Please read aloud)
_____
_____
_____

All of us have been physically born through our parents. However, Jesus is talking about a spiritual birth. Only those who will believe & receive will be able to enter the Kingdom of God.

Those who don't receive won't enter His Kingdom. He makes it very clear. Being a Christian is not about what denomination you are part of currently. It's all about believing & receiving the Spirit of God. Verse 8 says, "born of the Spirit" and verse 3 says "born again".

C. Write down John 6:44 and read verses 43-47
_____
_____

Jesus is saying in verse 44 that you can't even come to God unless he draws you. That is what God is doing right now through this lesson. You are hearing and learning of Him and He is drawing you right now.

D. Write down John 6:47 (Please read aloud)
_____
_____

E. There are 3 simple words that God asks you to do to obtain everlasting life. What are they? _____

F. Write down John 3:16 (Please read aloud)
_____
_____
_____

There were several scriptures that you read that spoke of believing on Jesus. Christianity is all about believing (having faith) and putting that faith into action by receiving. All throughout the Bible you'll read that everywhere Jesus went personally or even where His Word was preached, miracles took place. When people came in contact with Jesus or even heard about Him, lives and lifestyles changed. This has been going on now for centuries. Men, women and children who believed and received were never the same.

G. Write down some names of relatives, friends, co-workers or neighbors you know who are true Christians. I'm not talking about just "churchgoers", but people who walk the walk not just talk the talk. Those are the ones who are born again. It's not about what denomination they are, it's about living a Godly lifestyle, having Godly morals, attitude and character.

_____
_____
_____
_____

NOTE: Christians aren't perfect but they don't intentionally sin. If they do mess up, they ask God's forgiveness immediately and determine with his help not to keep in sin.

The Bible is full of people whose lives and lifestyles changed by the love and forgiveness of our heavenly Father. We're going to read about a man who had a great life and chose to go do his own thing. I guess he thought he was missing out in life by the socalled fun he was probably hearing about. Read Luke 15: 11-24, the story of the "Prodigal Son".

Definition of **PRODIGAL:**
Recklessly extravagant, characterized by wasteful expenditure

When I looked up this word it gave this story more meaning. His story we all can relate to. Prior to being born again, we all have wasted our life that God gave us. I'm not talking about just those of us who have been addicted to something.

H. Write down Luke 15:17

_____
_____
_____

I. What do those first 6 words mean to you and can you relate?

_____
_____
_____
_____

This man messed up like we all have and fell into all kinds of sin that brought him terrible consequences. He did something though that many never do. He didn't let pride keep him from the one that loved him.

J. Write down Luke 15:18

_____
_____
_____

K. Do you believe as this man did, if you arise and go to your Heavenly Father that life for you will be better then it is now? Are you sick and tired of living at a lower standard than what your Father has waiting for you? Please write your thoughts on this.

_____
_____
_____

L. In verse 20, what was the Father's response to this disobedient son?

_____

If you want to make a U-Turn in life there is hope, love, and forgiveness waiting on you. Your heavenly Father is waiting for you to *believe and receive* today!

M. Write down verse 24 (Please read aloud)

_____
_____

Definition of **LOSE:**
Bring to destruction; to suffer loss or separation from; fail to keep control of or allegiance of; fail to use; let slip; fail to win, gain or obtain; undergo defeat; fail to keep, maintain or sustain; to wander or go astray from; fail to keep in mind or sight; to free oneself, get rid of, fail to advance or improve.

Definition of **LOST:**

Not made use of, won or claimed; unable to find the way; lacking assurance or self-confidence; ruined or destroyed physically or morally; no longer known; taken away or beyond reach; hardened; insensible.

Definition of **FIND:**
To come upon by searching; effort to gain or regain the use or power of; a valuable item of discovery

Definition of **RECOVER:**
To get back to normal position or condition; rescue, to reclaim; obtain a final legal judgment in one's favor; to recover again or renew.

Jesus said in Luke 19:10, "For the Son of Man is come to seek and to save that which was ***LOST***." If you had asked me before I was born again if I was lost, I would have said, are you crazy? I would have said I know where I'm at and what I'm doing. The old song *Amazing Grace* says it perfectly. We were spiritually blinded by the devil's lies but praise the wonderful name of Jesus he never gives up on us and seeks us out. His Holy Spirit draws us to believe and receive. Of course he leaves the choice to us. We have a free will. In verse 18-19, the son put his faith in action. In verse 20-21, he arose and went to the Father confessing he'd sinned.

When we believe and receive the Lord Jesus, a spiritual miracle happens. His Holy Spirit comes to live within us, empowering us to live a Godly lifestyle. Through this lesson, I hope you are able to see that the spiritual birth, being born again, was what was missing in our lives in order to overcome all of our addictions and sin. When we, by our choice and wholehearted commitment, dedicate our lives to God we are miraculously changed through Jesus Christ.

N. Write 2 Corinthians 5:17   (Please read aloud)
_____
_____
_____

The Lord gave us some awesome scriptures to show us that we *do* have the power to live a Godly lifestyle.

O. Write out Philippians 4:13   (Please read aloud)

_____

_____

P. Write out 2 Timothy 1:7   (Please read aloud)

_____

_____

Q. Write out Psalm 27:1   (Please read aloud)

_____

_____

_____

R. Write out Romans 8:37   (Please read aloud)

_____

_____

As you can see from these scriptures, God empowers us so that we can be changed. We can have a Godly lifestyle and be free. The reason we could not obtain and maintain an addiction or sin-free lifestyle is due to not believing & receiving the Holy Spirit. By our choice and wholehearted commitment, we dedicate our lives to God, through Jesus Christ. If you are ready to put your faith in action, say this simple prayer aloud. The Bible tells us in Romans 10:9-10 that "if you confess with your mouth and believe in your heart (this is a partial verse) you will be saved."

Say this prayer aloud: Jesus, I do believe you died for my sins and all my addictions so I could be your child, forgiven and free. I'm sorry for wasting the life you gave me. Please forgive me Jesus. I'm willing to leave my old lifestyle behind and begin my new lifestyle, today. I accept your forgiveness. I now receive your Holy Spirit that will empower me to live a Godly lifestyle. Thank you that I now have a clean conscience, free from all addiction and sin. I love you Jesus!   AMEN

Reference Section for Believe & Receive

A. John 1:12 But as many as received Him, to them gave He power to become the sons of God, even to them that believe on His name.

B. John 3:3 Jesus answered and said unto him, Verily, verily, I say unto thee, except a man be born again he cannot see the Kingdom of God.

C. John 6:44 No man can come to me, except the Father which hath sent me draw him: and I will raise him up at the last day.

D. John 6:47 Verily, verily, I say unto you, He that believeth On Me hath everlasting life.

E. Believeth on Me

F. John 3:16 For God so loved the world, that He gave his only begotten Son, that whosoever believeth in Him should not perish, but have everlasting life.

H. Luke 15:17 And when he came to himself, he said How many hired servants of my father's have bread enough and to spare and I perish with hunger!

J. Luke 15:18 I will arise and go to my father, and will say unto him, father, I have sinned against Heaven and before thee.

L. He had compassion on him.

M. For this my son was dead, and is alive again; He was lost, and is found. And they began to be merry.

N. 2 Corinthians 5:17 Therefore if any man be in Christ, he is a new creature: old things are passed away; behold, all things have become new.

O. Philippians 4:13 I can do all things through Christ which strengtheneth me.

P. 2 Timothy 1:7 For God hath not given us the spirit of fear; but of power, and of love, and of a sound mind.

Q. Psalm 27:1 The Lord is my light and my salvation; whom shall I fear? The Lord is the strength of my life; of whom shall I be afraid?

R. Nay, in all these things we are more than conquerors through Him that loved us.

Self-will or God's will

Lesson 3
Romans 10:9-10
COMMIT our life to God through Jesus Christ

A. Please write down Romans 10:9-10 (Please read aloud)

_____
_____
_____
_____
_____
_____
_____

Definition of **WILL:**
The mental faculty, by which one deliberately chooses, decides upon a course of action, volition; deliberate intention or wish; free discretion. The power to arrive at one's own decisions and to act upon it independently (in spite of oppositions.); determination; diligent purposefulness; self-control; self-discipline; To decree or make a firm choice.

B. What do the words "Mental Faculty" refer to? _____

C. Have you ever said or thought, "no one's going to tell me what to do"? Have you ever said, "I'm my own boss and I'll do as I please", not regarding at all someone's feelings or what the consequences will be? _____

Definition of **DELIBERATE:**
To ponder issues and decisions carefully, characterized by awareness of the consequences, resulting from careful and thorough consideration.

Definition of **PONDER:**

To weigh in the mind, to think about, consider, meditate, prolonged thinking about a matter

Definition of **MEDITATE:**
Focusing one's thoughts on something so as to understand it deeply

Definition of **VOLITION:**
An act of willful choosing or deciding by conscious choice; the power or capability of choosing

Ever since the Garden of Eden, God has given us free will, the ability to choose to either love, honor and obey Him or choose to do whatever we want. It has always been our choice and still is.

D. Please write down Proverbs 14:12   (Please read aloud)
_____
_____
_____

Lesson one pertains to acknowledging that we all are sinners. Through reading God's word, the Bible, we have received knowledge that God has made a way for us to become righteous through His Son, Jesus Christ. Prior to this knowledge, we all have been doing what Proverbs 14:12 says. Many have tried to live morally by using their own standards of right and wrong. Some have not taken such drastic destructive paths as others. I, Kandi Rose, the author, used my own freewill of choice that led me into multiple addictions that brought me not only great heartache, but affected many around me by my lifestyle. As we have read from the scriptures, even seemingly good, moral people are sinners and need to be born again just as much as anyone else on earth.

Definition of **MORAL:**
Relating to principles of right and wrong in behavior; operative on one's conscience or ethical judgment, having the effects of such on the mind, conscience or will

Definition of **RIGHTEOUS:**
Acting in accord with divine or moral law, free from guilt or sin, morally right or justifiable

As we read from Proverbs 14:12, we all have our own standard of what we think is right or wrong. So everyone who sincerely wants to live a good, clean life really cannot do so unless they do it God's way. That is why in order for us to live truly "Clean & Free" we must follow our road map, the Bible. God sent His Son, Jesus Christ to make us righteous by the blood sacrifice of Jesus Christ.

E. Please write down Isaiah 64:6   (Please read aloud)
_____
_____
_____

F. There is a key word that precedes the word righteousness. What is that word? _____

Can you see from these scriptures that people who seem to have good morals, who are not criminals or been addicted to any destructive behavior are still not good enough by God's standards? The Good News is: God's will and way was provided for us at Calvary.
We are going to now look at Jonah's life and see what happened to him when he disobeyed God's instruction.

Read all 4 Chapters of the book of Jonah.

We can learn a lot from Jonah's life about the topic of self-will vs. God's will. Jonah did not want to do what God wanted him to do (just like we all have done at one time or another). He went through much needless suffering. It almost cost him his life and the lives of those around him. We can certainly apply his experiences to our own life and hopefully help us avoid the same mistakes.

G. In Jonah 1:2, what are the first 2 words God said to Jonah?

H. We're no better than Jonah. We have not always done what God is prompting us to do. We're real good at procrastinating or making excuses why we can or can't do what he's urging us to do.

What happened to Jonah when he let self-will take over? Read Jonah 1:4–17 and write down what happened as the result of his disobedience.

_____
_____
_____

I. Tremendous consequences followed when he disobeyed the voice of the Lord. While he was going through this terrifying experience, what was Jonah's response? What did he do in 2:2?

_____

J. In Jonah 2:3, he acknowledged something. It's found in the first part of the verse. Write down this important statement of Jonah's. The reason of its importance is because if he had never acknowledged, he never would have gotten free. He would have died in that whale's belly.

_____
_____

K. Just as he felt there was no hope and he was at his lowest emotionally and physically, what did he do? Fill in the blanks with 2 key words taken from 2:7. "When my soul fainted within me I, _____ the Lord and my _____ came in unto thee, into thine Holy Temple." He believed God could make a difference.

L. Jonah's body was not only undergoing severe stress but so was his mind. Write out Jonah 2:5

_____
_____
_____

M. Are you now or have you in the past felt like you were in a whale's belly?_____ Have you ever been under severe stress physically or emotionally that you knew was a definite result of your sin or addiction? Not all afflictions are a direct result from our own doing. I understand that some of our hardships in life are a result of another person's choice and they will answer to God for someday. Write down some sin choices that you made that caused great havoc in not only your life but also in others.

_____
_____
_____
_____
_____

N. In Jonah 2:9, Jonah surrendered himself over to God's will. He was now willing to not only make but keep his commitment. Write out this verse and ask yourself, "am I ready?" He's been waiting for your commitment and your vow of love to Him.

_____
_____
_____

God has given us His Word, the Holy Bible as our road map to living our daily lives. It tells us what to do and what not to do. How to act, talk and walk that would please Him. We can know what God's will is by not only reading his Word but by listening to his voice through the Holy Spirit given to us when we make a commitment. Born again! We'll have no excuse because Jesus Christ died to give us power over sin. We *can* do God's will and not just our own.

Will you choose to follow His voice of Love calling you? Will you allow him to love you and you love him in return?

Eve let the devil influence her mind and free will. It's time to take a stand and confess with your mouth that you choose to accept His love and desire to do His will. When Jesus died on that cross, giving his life's blood for us, He took back that power and authority for us to be able to do God's will. We now can have victory and power! Addiction and sin is under the blood through the powerful name of Jesus Christ!

If you want to do God's will and not your own anymore, just cry out to him just like Jonah did and pray a vow of commitment. Write out a simple prayer using these 3 principles to guide you:

1: Acknowledge you're a sinner and that you've not been living your life according to His standards that are found in His Word, the Holy Bible.

2: Tell him you **believe** he can make a difference, giving you a new life.

3: Tell your heavenly Father that you believe Jesus Christ died on the cross for your sins, and ask him to forgive you. Tell him **you're willing to leave your old lifestyle and your self-will in the past.**

Write down your prayer to *acknowledge* him as your Savior, *believing and receiving* him as your Good Shepherd. Tell him you want to *surrender all* your old lifestyle, letting him guide you as a Shepherd does his sheep._____
_____
_____
_____
_____
_____
_____
_____

Jesus loves you so much! He's been trying to get your love and devotion for a long time. The devil has lied to you long enough. Listen to His voice of love calling you today.

Recovery Today & Everyday! The Shepherd's Way

Reference Section for Self-Will or God's Will

A. Romans 10:9-10 That if thou shalt confess with thy mouth the Lord Jesus, and shalt believe in thine heart that God hath raised him from the dead, thou shalt be saved. For with the heart man believeth unto righteousness; and with the mouth confession is made unto salvation.
B. Mind
C. Yes
D. Proverbs 14:12 There is a way which seemeth right unto a man, but the end thereof are the ways of death.
E. Isaiah 64:6 But we are ALL as an unclean thing, and all our righteousness are as filthy rags; and we all do fade as a leaf; and our iniquities, like the wind, have taken us away.
F. Our
G. Arise, Go
I. He cried unto the Lord
J. He reasoned, acknowledged, his problems were because of his disobedience.
K. Remembered, prayer
L. The waters compassed me about, even to the soul: the depth closed me round about, the weeds were wrapped about my head.
M. Yes
N. Jonah 2:9 But I will sacrifice unto thee with the voice of thanksgiving; I will pay that that I have vowed. Salvation is of the Lord.

X-Treme Character Makeover

Lesson 4
Psalm 51:6
EXAMINE destructive actions and inward attitudes

A. Write out Psalm 51:6 (Please read aloud)
_____
_____
_____

CHARACTER refers to:
Moral qualities and ethical standards that make up the inner nature of a person

PERSONALITY refers to:
Particularly to outer characteristics that determine the impression that a person makes upon others

TRAIT refers to:
Characteristic, quality, attribute, feature

BEHAVIOR refers to:
The manner of conducting oneself, involving action and response, to manage the actions of oneself in a particular way, conduct

CONDUCT refers to:
Action or behavior that shows the extent of one's power to control or direct oneself

Prior to surrendering our lives to Jesus Christ and making Him our higher power, we did not have very good behavior. Many of us had some good character traits but we acquired some very destructive behavior patterns called addiction and sin.

As young children we are born with a unique personality that God created us to have. So unique that there is no one else on this earth created exactly as we are. As we studied the scriptures, we found out that we were born with a sinful nature because of the first man on earth, Adam. We also learned that we can attain a new nature to empower us to change those old behaviors through receiving the Holy Spirit. When we chose to dedicate our life to God, through Jesus Christ, we then became born again, given a new spiritual nature.

God created us to be His Family, children that he could have a relationship with, as an object of His love and affection. It's the same reason we have for wanting children.

B. Write down Revelation 4:11   (Please read aloud)
_____
_____
_____

C. Why did He create all things? _____

As we read from scriptures previously, upon receiving the Holy Spirit, we become empowered to live a Godly lifestyle. God is Holy and cannot have companionship with mankind because of sin. That is why God sent Jesus Christ, our higher power, to die for us. Christ's blood was shed enabling us to become righteous, holy, and sanctified. The Holy Spirit came to live inside our bodies to sanctify us. We now are holy in God's sight, not because of anything good we have done, but because of what Jesus Christ has already done on the cross.

D. Read I Corinthians 6:9-20 and write down verse 19
_____
_____
_____

(Please read verse 19 aloud)
As we have read, our body is a temple (church) where the Holy Spirit lives. This is why it's so important to allow God's Spirit to do a house cleaning or "sanctify" us of all the garbage of sin and addiction.

We become sanctified the moment we dedicate our life to Jesus. Then a **process starts taking place** that will be life-long on this earth, called sanctification. A simpler term would be called spiritual growth. Just as a newborn baby grows physically, so we too who have been born again spiritually must now grow into a Godly person. Through reading God's Word, we can learn how to live a pleasing and acceptable lifestyle to God.

E. Write the scripture John 17:17   (Please read aloud)
_____
_____

F. How do we become sanctified? _____

Definition of **SANCTIFY:**
To set apart for a (sacred purpose) or religious use, to free from sin, purify,

Definition of **SANCTIFICATION:**
The state of growing in divine grace as a result of Christian commitment after conversion

(Please read aloud I Thessalonians 4:1-7)
The word vessel refers to your body where the Holy Spirit lives once you make a commitment to live for Jesus.

G. Write out I Thessalonians 4:4   (Please read aloud)
_____
_____

H. Write out I Thessalonians 4:7   (Please read aloud)
_____
_____

I. According to those scriptures what is the purpose of sanctification? _____
In verse 3 God uses the word, **"ABSTAIN".** In that verse, He gives only one example of the many habits and behaviors we are to not engage in.

Synonyms for **ABSTAIN:**
Refrain, give up, withdraw, go without; don't indulge in

In verse 3, God tells us that we "should", and in verse 4 we "should know how". This indicates that it's up to us to take action. God has provided the source of power through the sanctifier, the Holy Spirit, so now we must take action and do what the Bible says.

J. Read James 1:19-27 and write verse 22 (Please read aloud)

_____

_____

Now that we have studied scriptures that tell us our bodies are a temple or a church where the Holy Spirit lives, let's look at another verse.

K. Write down I Corinthians 3:17 (Please read aloud)

_____

_____

_____

Definition of **DEFILE:**
To make unclean or impure, to corrupt the purity or perfection of; to violate the chastity of; to make physically unclean with something unpleasant or contaminating, to violate the sanctity of, dishonor, desecrate

Definition of **SANCTITY:**
Holiness of life and character, Godliness

Remember the word defile means **"to violate the sanctity of."**

L. Upon reading I Corinthians 3:17, we should see how important it is *what* we put in our minds and bodies. What did God say he would do if we defiled our temple? _____

That should make us want to obey His instructions!

M. Honestly write down what you have allowed to defile your temple, your mind and body.

_____
_____
_____

There's good news, of course, that all those things can be changed by the power of the Holy Spirit. It's not our own self-will that changes us, producing Godly character. It's by God giving us the Holy Spirit (the sanctifier) to live within us that empowers us to daily live a holy, Godly lifestyle. Since God has sent Jesus to die for us, we can live Godly. We will have no excuse when we stand before him someday face to face. He loves us and wants you and me to know this truth so we can have a good life not only on this earth but go to heaven to live with Him forever.

N. The devil wants to destroy you, but read, write and memorize this important scripture John 10:10   (Please read aloud)

_____
_____
_____

As you can see by the scriptures we studied, God desires to give us an X-Treme Character Makeover. Just as parents have to set guidelines and boundaries of what behavior is or isn't acceptable, so does God using the Bible as our road map Just as we tolerate or not tolerate certain behaviors, why do we think we can just act & do whatever we feel like and God won't care? Behavior is important! God expects us to find out what is acceptable or not acceptable behavior by reading His Word, the Bible.

O. Read 2 Timothy 2:19-26 and write out verse 15:

_____
_____
_____

P. Read 2 Timothy 2:21 and write down the reason God wants to sanctify us.

Upon receiving this wonderful truth, would you now like to have God continue this wonderful process called sanctification? If so, just say a simple prayer like this:

Father God, thank you for sending your Son, Jesus, to die on the cross for me. Thank you for sending the Holy Spirit to enable me to change my old actions & attitudes. I want to be a vessel of honor as I represent you to others who are lost without you. Use my life now as I choose to obey your Word. Thank you for never giving up on me and loving me even with my unlovable behaviors. Your unconditional love overwhelms me. Even though you loved me in my sinful state, you loved me enough to not let me live and die like that. Thank you for pursuing me with your love.

The world is watching the lives of people who profess to be Christians. I'm sorry to say that many people's lives have not lined up with their profession as they observe their actions & attitudes. Therefore, because many "talk the talk" but do not "walk the walk", it causes others to not even want to be a Christian. Let us not be a bad example, but strive to grow spiritually through sanctification.

There's an old saying, "Christians aren't perfect, just forgiven." That is true but many use that as an excuse to sin and then ask forgiveness over and over again. The truth is, Christians don't intentionally sin but we all are in a continual, sanctification, growing process.

Q. Write down I John 2:6 (Please read aloud)

_____

Let's all ask the Lord to make us more like our example, Jesus Christ. Before every decision let us ask ourselves, "Would Jesus

Do this?" Would Jesus "*Say this*?" Would Jesus "*Go there*?" Would Jesus "*Watch this*?" Would Jesus "*Partake in this*?" He is Holy and he expects us to live holy lives as well. In your life's journey, you will not be as perfect as Jesus, but we can strive to become more like Him every day. That is why Jesus died on the Cross so that we can overcome through the power of the Holy Spirit.

R. Read I John 1:4-10 and 2:1-7, then write verse 1:9
___
___
___

Enjoy your life as a Christian now and let His love and compassion in you reach out to all the many people God will put in your path as His messenger. What the devil meant for bad in your life will be used to help others since, "you've been there – done that" and didn't like it!

When you ask God to forgive you, He does! So don't stay under guilt & condemnation. If you're willing, he'll show you daily what home improvements need to be made in your life. As you allow Him to remove those character flaws *SIN,* you will enjoy life and be greatly used by God. It's an awesome feeling!

S. Write out Romans 8:1 (Please read aloud and memorize)
___
___
___

You can brag on Jesus like the author of this book does. We are not like we used to be, and by the power of the Holy Spirit we will allow Him to continue His process.

Recovery Today
& Everyday!

Reference Section for
X-Treme Character Makeover

A. Psalm 51:6 Behold, thou desirest truth in the inward parts: and in the hidden part thou shalt make me know wisdom.
B. Revelation 4:11 Thou art worthy O Lord, to receive glory and honor and power: for Thou hast created all things, and for Thy pleasure they are and were created
C. For His pleasure
D. What? Know ye not that your body is the temple of the Holy Ghost which is in you, which ye have of God, and ye are not your own?
E. John17:17 Sanctify them through Thy truth: Thy Word is truth.
F. Truth. Thy Word is truth (the scriptures, the Bible)
G. I Thessalonians 4:4 That every one of you should know how to possess his vessel in Sanctification and Honor. (Possess means to control or manage) (Vessel, is our body)
H. I Thessalonians 4:7 For God hath not called us unto uncleanness, but unto holiness.
I. To enable us to live a Godly lifestyle
J. James 1:22 But be ye doers of the Word, and not hearers only, deceiving your own selves.
K. I Corinthians 3:17 If any man defile the temple of God, him shall God destroy; for the temple of God is Holy, which temple ye are.
L. Destroy It
N. The thief cometh not, but for to steal, and to kill and to destroy; I am come that they might have life, and that they might have it more abundantly.
O. Study to shew thyself approved unto God, a workman that needeth not to be ashamed, rightly dividing the Word of truth.
P. God wants to use our life. So we must walk the walk and not just talk the talk.
Q. I John 2:6 He that saith he abideth in Him ought himself also so to walk, even as He walked
R. I John 1:9 If we confess our sins, He is faithful and just to forgive us our sins, and to cleanse us from all unrighteousness.
S. There is therefore now no condemnation to them which are in Christ Jesus, who walk not after the flesh, but after the Spirit.

Sharing-The Healing Begins

Lesson 5
Galatians 6:2
SHARE with others what has happened in your life

A. Write down Galatians 6:2   (Please read aloud)
_____
_____

Synonym for **BEAR**:
Endure (suffer, go through, abide), support (uphold, accept) assume (shoulder, carry, take on)

Synonym for **BURDEN:**
Load (problem), weight (heaviness)

Why is there suffering that causes us to have burdens problems, worries, and pain? Is there an invisible spiritual realm? Are there evil spirits? Is there a Holy Spirit and angels? Do our choices have consequences and do our choices affect our destiny? We have an enemy, Satan. In step 4, we read the scripture John 10:10 and saw that the devil's purpose is to steal, kill and destroy God's creation. In that same verse Jesus said, he's come to give life and life more abundantly.

We need to quit blaming God and see who our enemy really is so that we can be healed and restored. As we check into the scriptures during this study, we'll be able to recognize the devil's tactics and how he operates. This will help prevent us from relapsing or backsliding, falling back into our old addictions and sin.

B. Read I Peter 5: 7-10 write verse 8 (Please read verse 8 aloud)
_____
_____
_____
_____

C. According to verse 8, who is your adversary?_____

Definition of **ADVERSARY:**
Enemy, foe, opposition, antagonist, opponent, rival, challenge

Where did our Enemy, Adversary, the Devil and Evil Spirits come from? Read Revelation 12:7-12. In these scriptures God is telling us that Michael the Archangel, along with good angels, fought against the devil and other angels that decided to rebel with him. So God had them cast out of heaven onto earth. Read Isaiah 14: 12-15 These scriptures tell us why there was war in Heaven. The devil's name is also Lucifer. He became very prideful and wanted to be like God (verse 14).

Since he is God's enemy, he is also our enemy. Thanks be to God though who from the very beginning provided a plan that we could defeat the devil (Gen 3). All through the Old Testament it was predicted a Savior would come who would die for our sins. When Jesus Christ died on that cruel cross for us he broke the power of sin's hold on us. That's why we can be free from any addiction or sin. That's why this lesson is being shared with you so that you will know the truth and the ***application*** of that truth will set you free!

D. Write out John 8:32 (Please read aloud and memorize)
_____
_____

E. Write down I Peter 5:9 (Please read aloud)
_____
_____
_____

F. Fill in the blanks of verse 9: "Whom _____ steadfast in the_____,knowing that the _____ _____ are accomplished in your brethren that are in the world.
The Lord expects us to resist. He wouldn't have told us that if He had not already provided the power and authority to do so by the Holy Spirit.

The meaning of **AFFLICTION:**
Suffering, pain, anguish, distress, agony, torment

The second part of verse 9 shows us why we should be able to share & bear our burdens with each other, so that we can be healed and help others as well! There are countless people in this world who have experienced some of the same issues that you have had in your past or present. It's the same devil, which throughout the centuries has been keeping people from the truth as he has set out to steal, kill and destroy God's prize possession, you and I! That is why we shouldn't be ashamed to share, as we all can relate in some form or fashion, and instead of being judgmental we can be compassionate. We all have been a victim to the Devil's lies, one way or another. So when we begin to share, we start the process of healing. As we learn the truth found in God's Word, "the Holy Bible", the devil's lies are exposed!

We found out from the Bible just how much God loves us (John 3:16) and how much the devil hates us (John 10:10). There has been and will be until the day we die an evil scheme to keep us from the one who loves us and died for us, Jesus Christ! This is why it's so important for us to ***Share and Care*** for one another.

G. Write and memorize Jeremiah 29:11 (Please read aloud)
_____
_____
_____

In this lesson along with the previous ones, I pray that you will now want to start, "***Sharing your Burdens.***" From scriptures we have studied, we see that all have sinned and we all have a *common enemy*. We have also seen from scriptures that we have a loving and forgiving God. Of course we have studied that once this Good News has been shared with us and we reject it, He will someday be our judge.

H. Write down I Peter 5:7 (Please read that verse aloud)
_____
_____

There's an old adage that says, "Everyone has a skeleton in his or her closet". It means that everyone has something about them that they don't want you to know. Guess what? God knows but yet loves you enough to want to see you not carry those Burdens around any more. He wants to, heal your broken heart and of course forgive you. ***Cast all your Cares on Him*!**

I. Fill in the blanks of verse James 5:16
_____ your _____ one to _____, and _____ one for _____, that _____ may be _____. The _____ fervent _____ of a _____ man availeth much.

J. Write down in your own words what you feel God is telling you throughout this step lesson.
_____
_____
_____

One of the greatest privileges in life is when God can use our past and present circumstances to help someone else - as we point them to the one who has helped us, Jesus!

K. Write down 2 Corinthians 1:4 (Please read aloud)
_____
_____
_____

As we allow God to comfort and help us with all our problems, he can then use us to tell others how He is able to do the same for them. I encourage you to read all of Isaiah 53. If anyone has ever "Been there done that", it was Jesus during his life on earth! He knows what pain and sorrow is! He experienced it first hand, physical as well as emotional.

L. Write down Isaiah 53:3-4 (Please read aloud)
_____
_____

_____
_____
_____
_____

Jesus gives you and I an awesome invitation to find rest and peace for the daily issues that we all face.

M. Write down Matthew 11:28-30 (Please read aloud)
_____
_____
_____
_____

Is there some burden, problem, sin, physical or emotional hurt you've been carrying? Most of us have suffered tremendous hurts in our past and even present circumstances. When we suppress those feelings, we walk around wounded and God wants to heal us. Jesus said that He came to heal the brokenhearted (Isaiah 61:1).

The one we share with first of course is God. He is the only one that is actually *able to do* something about our problems. Then, as we learned in James 5:16, we should ***Share our Burdens*** with other Christians so that they can have the awesome privilege of praying with us. Pastors and Evangelists are not the only ones God uses to pray for people. You and I, along with other born again Christians, can pray for others and ***Expect Results!***

N. Write down I John 3:22 (Please read aloud)
_____
_____
_____

We have now seen in the scriptures that whether we pray by ourselves or have others pray for us, we can ***Expect God To Meet our Needs.*** Remember, prayer is talking and listening to God just as if you were speaking to a visible person. It's about a personal relationship with your Heavenly Father and Counselor who loves you.

O. Write down Isaiah 9:6. This verse predicted Jesus' birth centuries before he was born. It also tells us of what He would be, not only to the world, but also to each of us personally.

_____
_____
_____
_____

P. There is a key word in that verse that proves he desires to Share our Burdens with him first and foremost. What is that key word? _____

Whether you are doing this lesson alone or with one or more people, *please share and let the healing begin*!

Write down the issues you've been so wounded by. If you don't have someone right now to verbally share them with, I encourage you to do so as soon as possible. Don't carry those burdens alone anymore. God cares and so do so many others. As you share, you'll be surprised how many others have similar issues as well. As you write this down and verbalize your hurts, your Heavenly father and Counselor is listening and watching. He loves you!

_____
_____
_____
_____
_____
_____
_____
_____
_____

After becoming a Christian, this is a life long process. In this life we will have heartaches and sorrows as we are still dealing with an enemy. The Good News is, the Holy Spirit is in us, God is on our side, and Jesus is our Counselor. Read all of John 16. In verse 7, Jesus tells us that He would send a Comforter. The person of the Holy Spirit is who and why we can stay strong and not yield to the old way of handling our stress and problems.

Talk to Jesus and as you share your issues, your heart will be healed and you will be able to help others recover as well. He can and will help you. *He has started a good work in you. (Philippians 1:6),* **Let him finish it!**

**RECOVERY is POSSIBLE
TODAY
& EVERYDAY!**

Reference Section for Sharing-The Healing Begins

A. Galatians 6:2 Bear ye one another's burdens, and so fulfill the law of Christ.
B. I Peter 5:8 Be sober, be vigilant, because your adversary the devil, as a roaring lion, walketh about, seeking whom he may devour
C. Devil
D. John 8:32 And ye shall know the truth, and the truth shall make you free.
E. I Peter 5:9 Whom resist steadfast in the faith, knowing the same afflictions are accomplished in your brethren that are in the world.
F. Resist, faith, same afflictions
G. For I know the thoughts I think toward you, saith the Lord, thoughts of peace. And not of evil, to give you an expected end.
H. I Peter 5:7 Casting all your care upon him; for he careth for you.
I. James 5:16 Confess *your* faults one to another, and pray one for another, that ye may be healed. The effectual fervent prayer of a righteous man availeth much
K. 2 Corinthians 1:4 who comforteth us in all our tribulation, that we may be able to comfort them which are in any trouble, by the comfort wherewith we ourselves are comforted of God
L. Isaiah 53:3-4 He is despised and rejected of men; a man of sorrows, and acquainted with grief: and we hid as it were our faces from him; he was despised, and we esteemed him not. Surely he hath borne our griefs, and carried our sorrows; yet we did esteem him stricken, smitten of God, and afflicted.
M. Matthew 11:28-30 Come unto me, all *ye* that labour and are heavy laden, and I will give you rest. Take my yoke upon you, and learn of me; for I am meek and lowly in heart: and ye shall find rest unto your souls. For my yoke *is* easy, and my burden is light.
N. I John 3:22 And whatsoever we ask, we receive of him, because we keep his commandments, and do those things that are pleasing in his sight.

O. Isaiah 9:6 For unto us a child is born, unto us a son is given; and the government shall be upon his shoulder: and his name shall be called wonderful, counselor, the mighty God, the everlasting father, the prince of peace.
P. Counselor

Rebellion or Submission

Lesson 6
Psalm 51:17
Be **WILLING** to turn from a lifestyle of sin

A. PS. 51:17 Please write and read out loud

_____
_____
_____

Definition of: **REBELLION**
Opposition to one in authority or dominance;
Open defiance or resistance; to oppose or disobey one in authority or control; to act in or show disobedience.

Definition of **SUBMISSION**:
To yield; to subject to the authority or will of another; to defer to the opinion or authority of another; humble; or compliant.

B. Write down I Samuel 15:23   (Please read that verse aloud)

_____
_____
_____
_____

C. Are you doing what God desires for your life? _____

D. Is He in control of *all* areas your life? _____

E. What areas specifically have you not been in submission to Him?

_____
_____
_____

F. Do you like it when you're in control of your life? _____

G. Have there been and will there be bad consequences if you continue to rebel? _____

H. Why do we rebel?
_____

I. What consequences could happen if we continue rebelling?
_____
_____
_____

MEANING OF **CONTRITE:**
Grieving and penitent for sin or shortcoming

MEANING OF **PENITENT:**
Expressing humble or regretful pain or sorrow for sins or offenses, repentant

MEANING OF **REPENT:**
To turn from one's sin and dedicate oneself to the amendment of one's life, to feel sorrow or regret or contrition for, to change one's mind.

J. Read Psalm 81:8-16 and write out verse 13
_____
_____

K. Read James 4:1-10 and write out verse 7
_____
_____

L. There are two key action words that God expects us to follow in verse 7. What are they? _____

M. What do you think God wants you to do pertaining to those 2 words? Write down some actions that you have already done or will do to be in submission to His will.
_____
_____

_____
_____
_____

N. The first 4 words of James 4 verse 8 tell us what?
_____

O. What types of action will you do to accomplish this command?
_____
_____
_____

P. James 4 verse 8 also tells us to _____ your _____, ye _____, and_____ your _____, ye _____.

Q. What do you think God is telling us in the rest of that verse? Write down your thoughts.
_____
_____
_____

It's our choice; will we submit to his authority and will? We can choose to rebel and do our own thing or we can choose to submit. Once we make a wholehearted decision, the miracle happens. The Holy Spirit comes inside us, empowering us to resist the devil. This is why all the good intentions we've had in the past to quit certain habits and attitudes failed. We lacked the power from the higher power, Jesus Christ.

R. Write out this very important scripture, John 1:12
_____
_____

This is a made up mind, not a half-hearted decision. It's the most important decision we'll ever make in our lives. This choice brings great rewards, not only in this life, but the life to follow in eternity.

Definition of **RESIST:**
Resist means to take a stand, to withstand the force or effect of; to exert oneself to counteract or defeat; to exert force in opposition.

So we see, once we make the choice, God expects us to do something: *to resist, to say no to sin.* That's why He died on the cross, to give us the power and ability to say no. We won't be able to have any excuse when we stand before God someday. He died to give us a new lifestyle and freedom from any type of sin or addiction.

S. Write II Cor.5:17 Please read aloud)

_____
_____
_____

T. Do you see from this scripture that choices of submission will ultimately result in a changed lifestyle?____ Your old addictions and sin, former choices of rebellion, will pass away, be gone.

That scripture says that all things have become new. Our new lifestyle will be one of submission, living according to his Word, and making good healthy choices.

U. Write down some *ways that you are going to resist sin.* What action plans are you going to make that will better enable you to not have that temptation always before you?

Remember God expects us to *do something* - **Resist**! He wouldn't tell us to do it if he thought we weren't capable. Writing this out will help you get that plan of action underway.

_____
_____
_____
_____
_____
_____

V. Most of us yield to temptations when under stress. We turn to our old ways of finding temporary peace. Write down some things you can do when these stressful circumstances arise.
_____
_____
_____
_____

**Do we want to submit to the devil and be in opposition to God?
Do we want to submit to God and be in opposition to the devil?**

Without realizing it, when there's no choice to submit to God, we've already submitted to the devil.

W. Read Matthew 6:24 and write it out
_____
_____
_____

X. Fill in the blanks taken from Joshua 24:14
_____ therefore _____ the Lord, and _____ him in _____ and in _____; and _____ away the _____, which your fathers served that were on the other side of the flood, and in Egypt; and _____ _____ the Lord.

Y. Those are key words that you wrote down. Please write down your thoughts of how that verse applies to you personally. Take each underlined word and ask yourself this question, "What is God teaching me and how does it apply to my daily life circumstances?"
_____
_____
_____
_____

Z. Fill in the blanks taken from Joshua 24:15
And if it seem evil unto you to serve the Lord, _____ _____ This day whom _____ will _____; whether the Gods which your fathers served that were on the other side of the flood, or the Gods of the Amorites, in whose land ye dwell; but as for _____ and _____ house, _____ will _____ the Lord.

When we read about the Israelites serving other Gods, we think in terms of idols and statutes. We turn to our addictions and sin to find comfort, pleasure, love, peace etc., instead of a loving God.

Now, read the entire book of Nehemiah.

NOTE: God sent Nehemiah to rebuild the broken down walls of Jerusalem. Walls brought shelter and protection from their enemies. We have a spiritual enemy. As we read these chapters, it will help us understand how God wants to *Rebuild, Restore and Recover our lives.*

Definition of **RESTORE:**
To give back something taken away or lost; to bring back health, strength; to bring back into being.

Definition of **REBUILD**
To make extensive changes in, reconstruct

Definition of **RECOVER:**
To get back something lost or stolen; regaining or reclaiming, to get back to a state of control, balance, or composure

In chapter 8 of Nehemiah, Ezra publicly read the scriptures to the people. In chapter 9 he tells them the story of how God used Moses to bring their ancestors out of their bondage in Egypt. He told of the miracles God performed such as parting the Red Sea for them to escape from their enemy. Even though they experienced all those miracles and were brought out to freedom, they still rebelled against God. Haven't we've done the same thing in our lives? God has done many miracles for us. Many of us have been spared from death, probably several times. I'm sure there were times when we weren't even aware of situations that almost happened.

Often, addictive lifestyles lead people into evil places and circumstances. God dispatched His angels to assist us many times. We just weren't aware there was a spiritual battle that was taking place for our heart, mind and soul. It was a battle between evil spirits and the Holy Spirit. As the Word of God was read and the Israelites learned the truth, they repented, turned from their sin and were happy!

AA. Write down some of the miracles God has done for you in your past, such as near death experiences, healings, provision of needs, family and friends, etc.

_____
_____
_____
_____
_____

BB. Write out Nehemiah 9:7

_____
_____

As we honestly take personal inventory of our actions and attitudes, God will help us. Submission sounds like weakness but on the contrary, great inner strength and power are the results. Power to resist temptation, addictions and sin of any kind, the power to say no to sin!

As we submit on a daily basis, healthy choices can be made based on God's Word, the Holy Bible, our road map for victorious living. We will no longer be in bondage, a slave to sin and addiction. We will be clean and free through submission to the one who loves us and died to set us free!

Through this study and reading the scriptures, do you see how God desires to give you a new life? He loves you so much and sees all the heartache you've been through. Possibly we didn't even realize that it was God we were rebelling against. We've been wounded people, who have acted out of hurt, who not only ended up hurting ourselves but all those around us.

It's time to allow God to heal our broken hearts and be in submission to the one who loves us, Jesus Christ, our higher power.

Commit your life to him with your whole heart right now and live a life of:

**RECOVERY TODAY
& EVERYDAY**

Reference section for Rebellion or Submission

A. Psalm 51:17 The sacrifices of God are a broken Spirit; a broken and a contrite heart, O God, thou wilt not despise.
B. I Samuel 15:23 For rebellion is as the sin of witchcraft, and stubbornness is as iniquity and idolatry. Because thou hast rejected the WORD of the LORD, He hath rejected thee from being king.
F. No
G. Yes
H. Pride, Ego, what others will think, when we enjoy our sin, etc.
I. Suffer more losses such as, relationships, job, health, sanity, jail, death, etc.
J. Psalm 81:13 Oh that my people had hearkened unto me, and Israel had walked in my ways!
K. James 4: 7 Submit yourselves therefore to God. Resist the devil, and he will flee from you."
L. Submit and Resist
N. Draw nigh to God
P. Cleanse, hands, sinners, purify, hearts, double minded
R. John 1:12 But as many as received him, to them gave he power to become the sons of God, even to them that believe on his name.
S. 2 Cor. 5:17 Therefore if any man be in Christ, he is a new creature: old things are passed away; behold, all things are become new.
T. Yes
U. Pray (talking to God), read your Bible, call a Christian, turn on Christian TV or Radio, Flee (get away from the temptation if possible)
V. Can be some of the answers in previous question; add more of your own if you can think of more.
W. Matthew 6:24 No man can serve two masters: for either he will hate the one, and love the other; or else he will hold to the one, and despise the other. ye cannot serve God and mammon.
X. Joshua 24:14 now, fear, serve, sincerity, truth, put, gods, serve ye"

Z. Joshua 24:15 Choose ye, ye, serve, me, my, we, serve"
BB. Nehemiah 9:17 And Refused to obey, neither were mindful of thy wonders that thou didst among them, but hardened their necks, and in their rebellion appointed a captain to return to their bondage: but thou art a God ready to pardon, gracious and merciful, slow to anger, and of great kindness, and forsookest them not."

Change or Same ole-Same ole

Lesson 7
I John 1:9
With humility we ask Jesus Christ to **CHANGE** us

A. Write down I John 1:9   (Please read aloud)

_____
_____
_____

In the scripture you just wrote, God promises to forgive us if we confess our sins and addictions. Let's look at some meanings of some very simple words to give us a deeper understanding of this verse and this step of the process.

Definition of **CONFESS:**
Admit, own up, acknowledge, come clean, declare

God is telling us if we confess we have sinned, violated his written laws in the Bible, he will forgive us. Remember when you were a child and your parent asked you if you did something wrong and you lied? When you didn't confess and kept denying it, didn't that make them upset? When God sees and knows everything we've ever done and when we keep acting like we're so good, don't you think that hurts him? Since God is holy and sin separates us from him, he wants us to own up to what he's already been seeing and hearing us do, so we can have a pure relationship with him.

He loves us and is not out to destroy us, but desires to restore us to him. When we, by our choice, deny his call of love to confess our sins, we ultimately ruin our own lives. This choice will determine our eternal destiny causing us to be separated from him after we die because he is a Holy God. Sin cannot have a pure relationship with a Holy God in this life or eternity. That's why he sent Jesus to save us from our sins by dying for us.

B. Write down 2 Peter 3:9   (Please read aloud)
_____
_____
_____
_____

Definition of **REPENT:**
To turn from sin and dedicate oneself to the amendment of one's life; to feel regret, sorrow or contrition, to change one's mind

Definition of **CHANGE:**
To make radically different, transform; to give a different direction, course or position to

Definition of **TRANSFORM:**
Change, convert, makeover, renovate

A transformation takes place in a person spiritually upon making a wholehearted choice, decision to turn our life over to Christ, letting him be the boss of our life. We've been lied to by our enemy Satan, and now need our thought life changed.

C. Write down Romans 12:1 & 2 (Please read aloud)
_____
_____
_____
_____
_____
_____
_____
_____
_____

D. In the last half of verse 2, what is the key word God tells us to do with our MINDS?_____

We do this is by reading and hearing the WORD of God. The Bible was written for us to be able to get to know God personally, to establish a relationship with him, and to find out how he expects us to live. We come to learn his character and realize as we read or hear a sermon he is speaking to us. He not only sees and hears us, but also loves us so very much. This is why it's so important we read our Bible often, go to Church, and of course take time each day with the one who loves you and died for you through prayer. All through the day remember to talk to him, as he's right by your side desiring your love and attention.

Synonym for **CHANGE:**
Alter, Modify, Vary

Definition of **ALTER:**
Implies a difference in some particular respect without changing the identity

When we come to God, we still have all the good qualities and talents he created us with. We don't lose our identity and become a robot that he manipulates. Using our freewill of choice, he gives us his precious Holy Spirit to help us to spiritually mature to become more like our example Jesus, our higher power.

Definition of **VARY:**
Vary stresses a breaking away from sameness, duplication, or exact repetition

Are you ready for a change?
Are you tired of the same
cycle of repetition in your life?

They say insanity is expecting different results when we aren't willing to do anything different that will bring about change.

We get stuck in a rut, just existing day to day. Dreams and goals become shattered as our habits and addictions continue to keep us from achieving the fulfilling life God has for us. When Satan, our enemy, continues to mess with our thought life, he keeps us from knowing the truth, and we continue in the same way of thinking and acting. We learned the meaning of repentance means a change of mind.

E. Write down Isaiah 1:18   (Please read aloud)
_____
_____
_____
_____
_____

F. In the first part of that verse, fill in the following, "Come now and let us _____

Definition of **REASON**:
The power of comprehending, inferring, or thinking; to take part in conversation or discussion; to talk with another so as to influence his actions or opinions so as to arrive at a conclusion

Wow! That should make us feel so loved and special to realize our Heavenly Father desires to talk to us. That verse is a plea to reason with us to change our minds. He desires to forgive us and set us free! We have come to the conclusion that our decisions determine our direction, and then our direction determines our destiny. Daily choices greatly determine our destiny. God gave us a free will. Prior to making a wholehearted choice to let Jesus Christ be in authority of our life, we lacked the power to not only make but also keep that decision. Once we seriously make that commitment and believe we then receive the Holy Spirit who enables us to walk the walk.

G. Write down 2 Timothy 3:16   (Please read aloud)
_____
_____
_____

H. Please write down the reasons God gave us the scriptures according to that verse.
_____
_____

Look at the last few words of that verse. Those words tell us the Word of God was also given for instruction in righteousness. That verse is telling us we need to be instructed, taught how to live a Godly lifestyle.

Definition of **RIGHTEOUSNESS:**
Virtue, morality, decency, uprightness, honesty

Definition of **RIGHTEOUS:**
Acting in accordance with divine or moral law; free from guilt or sin

I. Write down Isaiah 64:6 (Please read aloud)
_____
_____
_____
_____

J. Please write down Proverbs 14:12 (Please read aloud)
_____
_____
_____

Most of our lives we have tried in our own power and strength to live morally right. We learned this verse before in another step lesson, but this verse reminds us again why we need Jesus to save us from our sins, causing us to become righteous. God wants to instruct us through hearing and reading his Word so that we can daily live in accordance to his divine law.

Before dedicating our life to Christ, we not only acted contrary to God's written Word but our thinking didn't line up to his ways. The way to get our minds renewed, changed, is by the Word of God.

Remember we were told in Isaiah 1:8 that God wants to reason with us, change our minds. When our thought life changes, our actions, habits and attitudes change. The results bring a new lifestyle, a Godly lifestyle. Let me ask you some questions. I feel

God is *reasoning* with you right now. I believe these questions will help you to have a change of mind, and a new way of thinking.

- Are you **willing to change**?
- Are there things in your life that are hurting not only you but also all those around you?
- Are you sick of this spiritual battle within that you will **do whatever it takes** to change?
- Are you ready to **seriously make that whole heart commitment** to allow God to make the change within you?
- Are you willing to lead a **disciplined lifestyle**?

God gives us the power but we must take the initiative! As we learned before, it is the Holy Spirit that supernaturally gives us the power to live holy. Now it's up to us to make some positive choices that will renew our thinking. Biblical thinking will ultimately give us the victory over our old way of thinking and acting including our attitudes.

K. Make a plan of action: What are you going to do now that will not only start you on the right path but also enable you to keep on living a Godly lifestyle? How are you going to get your mind renewed? Ask others for their input if you'd like.

_____
_____
_____
_____
_____
_____
_____
_____

Expect, Expect, Expect! God is going to do great things in you and through you if you've made that decision. As you continue to progress, there will be trials and temptations. Remember, who you are now and to whom you belong. Trust your Good Shepherd to guide and direct you every day.

Get excited because living for Jesus is an adventure! Don't let up on your action plan ever! It will keep you from going back to your old lifestyle.

**Recovery is possible!
Today & Everyday**

Reference section for Change or Same Ole-Same Ole

A. I John 1:9 If we confess our sins, He is faithful and just to forgive US our sins, and to cleanse us from all unrighteousness.
B. 2 Peter 3:9 The Lord is not slack concerning his promise, as some men count slackness; but is longsuffering to usward, not willing any should perish, but that all should come to repentance.
C. Romans 12:1-2 I beseech you therefore, brethren, by the mercies of God, that ye present your bodies a living sacrifice, Holy, acceptable unto God, which is your reasonable service. And be not conformed to this world: but be ye transformed by the renewing of your mind that ye may prove what is that good and acceptable, and perfect, will of God.
D. Renew
E. Isaiah 1:18 Come now, and let us reason together saith the Lord: though your sins be as scarlet, they shall be as white as snow; though they be red as crimson, they shall be as wool.
F. Reason together
G. 2 Timothy 3:16 all scripture is given by inspiration of God, and is profitable for doctrine, for reproof, for correction, for instruction in righteousness.
H. Doctrine, Reproof, Correction, and Instruction in Righteousness
I. Isaiah 64:6 But we are all as an unclean thing, and all our righteousness are as filthy rags; and we all do fade as a leaf; and our iniquities, like the wind, have taken us away.
J. Proverbs 14:12 There is a way that seemeth right unto a man, but the end thereof are the ways of death.

I'm Sorry brings Peace

Lesson 8
Matthew 5:23-24
RECONCILE with those we hurt in the past & present

A. Write down Matthew 5:23-24 (Please read aloud)

_____
_____
_____
_____
_____

Prior to Jesus dying on the cross, people brought animal sacrifices to the altar as a gift to God to pay for their sins. Jesus came to this world as the perfect Lamb of God to be slaughtered as a sacrifice for our sins. We read in another lesson in Romans 12:1 that now we present our bodies as a gift to God, holy and acceptable to him. When Jesus died on the cross for you and I he reconciled us to God. God is Holy and sin separated us from Him. He expects us to do what He did, forgive. He forgave those that tortured and killed him. In those two verses, he is expecting us to do as he did. Forgiveness is a requirement, a command. In that verse God is telling us that since we no longer bring animals as a gift to the altar, we must present ourselves. He won't accept us until we reconcile, make peace with those we've offended.

B. Write down Matthew 6:14-15 (Please read aloud)

_____
_____
_____
_____

This lesson is not just about forgiving others, but asking those we've offended to forgive us. We may have allowed the Lord to help us forgive someone, but there may be someone who needs to hear us express our remorse to him or her. Matthew 5:23 is referring to a person having ought, offense against you. The Lord is telling us is that if you want forgiveness and a pure relationship with him we must go and make amends with others first.

Meaning of **OFFEND**:
To do wrong; to cause pain, hurt; to cause injury, difficulty or discomfort

Meaning of **OFFENSE:**
Wrongdoing, fault, crime, sin, felony, transgression, misdemeanor

Meaning of **FAULT:**
To blame, guilty, responsible

Meaning of **RECONCILE:**
Settle, resolve, merge, patch up, bring together, reunite

C. What are the two hardest words to say to someone when trying to reconcile? _____

Meaning of **SORRY:**
Apologetic, Regretful, Remorseful, Repentant

Meaning of **APOLOGY:**
Admission of guilt; request for forgiveness

Meaning of **REPENT:**
To turn from your present course of action; more than feelings of regret, but actions

It's so much easier to acknowledge others offenses toward us than to accept the fact we have people in our life that we have offended, either verbally, emotionally, physically or sexually. We tend to minimize or justify, what we did and why we did it, putting the blame on someone else. We may have offended or hurt someone who really did hurt us. There were also people who were innocent victims of our actions. At times, we have offended because of our own past hurts and memories from being a victim of others' sin choices against us. Regardless, Jesus is our example of why we should ask or extend forgiveness. Prior to Jesus dying on the cross, one of the most important statements he made was found in the Bible.

D. Write down Luke 23:34   (Please read aloud)
_____
_____
_____

Have you ever wondered why he made that statement? I know one of the main reasons was to show us this is how we are to live, daily forgiving. Christians, even with their new spiritual nature, tend to listen to the voice of the enemy. He urges us to react negatively when someone hurts our feelings or perpetrates even worse offenses such as physical, financial, or sexual harm. Forgiveness is a choice! Whose voice are we going to listen to, the voice of the devil or The Good Shepherd's voice?

God knew at the beginning of creation that mankind would have a sinful nature due to Adam and Eve's disobedience. People would inflict acts of cruelty toward each other. The first example of unforgiveness and resentment is when one of Adam & Eve's sons, Cain, killed his brother Abel.

Jesus was willing to come to earth and die for you and I to save us from this sinful nature that causes such destructive behavior. When Jesus died for our sins, that old sinful, destructive nature was defeated. Jesus set us free by giving us his new spiritual nature that we know as the Holy Spirit. We now have the capacity to be able to not only forgive those who victimized us but for us not to victimize anyone else in the future.

E. Do you see how important it is for us to not only forgive others, but to ask others to forgive us? Ask God to direct you to anyone *that you need to reconcile with* today. Everyone in this world has hurt someone, somehow, someplace, in his or her lifetime. Make a list of who and what offenses you did to them. No one has to see this list, except you and God. God of course already knows as he saw and heard it when it occurred. This list will help you and others receive the inner healing that God wants to perform. Jesus said that he came to heal the brokenhearted. This next section is for you to write down their names and the circumstances.

_____
_____
_____
_____
_____
_____
_____
_____

I, Kandi Rose, the author of this book made my own list that was very lengthy. I wrote an autobiography of my life that revealed I had been victimized many, many times. In that book I shared how I had also been a person who had victimized as well. In my book, I could not tell other horrible things I had done due to it causing some of my family more shame than they had experienced already. You can do this on a separate sheet of paper and then tear it up. Then ask God to forgive you. He will. I John 1 verse 9 Do what you can to make amends to people. Sometimes it's impossible due to the person having moved or passed away. If we are truly sorry, our guilt and shame can be removed once and for all through our forgiving Savior.

F. Write down Proverbs 28:13 (Please read aloud)

_____
_____
_____

G. Write down Psalm 86:5 (Please read aloud)

_____
_____
_____

H. Write down Psalms 103:12 (Please read aloud)

I. Write down and memorize I John 1:9 (Please read aloud)

J. Write down Isaiah 43:25 (Please read aloud)

K. After reading all those scriptures, what do you think God is telling you about your offenses against others? _____

He knows if we're truly sorry as he knows the intent of our heart and he will not only forgive you but forget as well. Of course after you have tried to make amends to some of those you've hurt and they don't accept it, don't be bitter. Remember that everyone is not where you are right now and begin to pray for him or her. God will help them just as he is helping you right now. You will at least have done what God has commanded you, to make peace with someone, reconcile, bring together, resolve, and reunite.

L. Write down Matthew 5:9 (Please read aloud)

We all have offended first and foremost, God. Sin of any kind is an offense against God himself. As we studied previously, this started in the Garden of Eden and since then, all of us are born with this offensive, disobedient, sin nature. Sin causes us to be an enemy of God, deserving his wrath and judgment. God in his great love for us sent Jesus, who willingly came to earth to die for us. At his death he reconciled us to God. He made peace between God and us! His shed blood made us holy and acceptable to a Holy God. Of course as we have read from so many scriptures this is a free gift. The choice is ours, whether to accept or reject this sacrificial act of love.

M. Read Romans 5:8-21 and write down verses 8-10

_____
_____
_____
_____

N. Write down Colossians 1:20-21

_____
_____
_____
_____
_____

Jesus, through his death, brought peace between God and us, reconciliation. Do you see now why he commands us to be reconciled to our fellow humans on this earth? It cost Jesus his very life's blood to be a peacemaker. Can we not make amends, and say, *"I'M SORRY"* to everyone we have offended and forgive those who have hurt us? Forgiveness is a huge issue to the Lord and it should become one of our top priorities as well. We must get rid of our anger, bitterness and resentment. When those things try to rear their ugly head and they will, deal with it immediately by talking to your heavenly Counselor, Jesus. He will help you through the power of the Holy Spirit. Jesus is our example of a peacemaker. We, too, must strive to be peacemakers.

O. Write down Acts 24:16

_____
_____
_____

Here is another example of the term, being offended. There will always be people who will be offended because of your belief in

Jesus Christ. Read Mark 6:3 and you will see people were offended because of who he was and whom he represented. When a person takes a stand for Jesus, they will offend many. Even your own family and friends may take offense. Jesus experienced this spiritual battle as well. Don't get angry. They're not rejecting you but Jesus!

I pray this lesson has begun a process of inner healing in not only your life, but in all those who have been affected by your choices. Many of us have been like the crowd that gathered to watch Jesus die. They didn't realize who Jesus really was, God, Emmanuel, God with us! That is why Jesus looked down from the cross and said, "Father forgive them, they know not what they do." He is saying that today, right now, to you and I. Since he extends this great love, mercy and forgiveness to us, let us make a choice to do the same.

Let's reconcile, make peace with God and man. Let us be peacemakers, as our example, Jesus, the Prince of Peace. Let forgiveness be a daily lifestyle.

If you have truly done this lesson with your whole heart, don't carry guilt and shame anymore. Jesus has forgiven you even if people haven't. No sin or offense is too bad that can't be forgiven. Jesus even forgave his tormentors. You are precious to the Lord. He died for you and all your sin and addictions of any kind.

P. Write down and memorize Romans 8:1

_____

_____

_____

God has allowed you to have access to these lessons to reveal his great love, mercy and forgiveness to you! Accept his free gift to you now and go on with your life. Be all God's created you to be and walk daily in his love.

Read this prayer aloud:

Jesus, I ask you to forgive me for all my sins. I'm truly sorry for all those that I have hurt through my own choices and lifestyle. I also forgive all those that have hurt me and my loved ones. I accept your great love, mercy and forgiveness. I want to let this be a daily lifestyle for me. I want to keep peace between you and I and with my fellow man. I'm willing to say, *I'VE DONE WRONG, I'M SORRY.*
Amen

Recovery Way is the Forgiving Way

Reference Section for
I'm Sorry brings Peace

A. Matthew 5:23-24 Therefore if thou bring thy gift to the altar, and there rememberest that thy brother hath ought against thee; Leave there thy gift before the altar, and go thy way; first be reconciled to thy brother, and then come and offer thy gift."
B. Matthew 6:14-15 For if ye forgive men their trespasses, your Heavenly Father will also forgive you: If ye forgive not men their trespasses, neither will your Father forgive your trespasses.
C. I'm sorry
D. Luke 23:34 Then said Jesus, Father, forgive them; for they know not what they do. And they parted his raiment, and cast lots.
F. Proverbs 28:13 He that covereth his sins shall not prosper: but whoso confesseth and forsaketh them shall have mercy.
G. Psalm 86:5 For thou, lord, art good, and ready to forgive; and plenteous in mercy unto all them that call upon thee.
H. Psalm 103:12 as far as the east is from the west, so far hath he removed our transgressions from us.
I. I John 1:9 If we confess our sins, he is faithful and just to forgive us our sins, and to cleanse us from all unrighteousness.
J. Isaiah 43:25 I, even I, am He that blotteth out thy transgressions for mine own sake, and will not remember thy sins.
K. Say I'm sorry
L. Matthew 5:9 Blessed are the peacemakers, for they shall be called the children of God.
M. Romans 5:8-10 But God commended his love toward us, in that, while we were yet sinners, Christ died for us. Much more then, being now justified by his blood, we shall be saved from wrath through him. For if, when we were enemies, we were reconciled to God by the death of his son, much more, being reconciled, we shall be saved by his life.
N. Colossians 1:20-21 and having made peace through the blood of his cross, by him to reconcile all things unto himself; by him, I say, whether they be things in earth, or things in heaven. And

you, that were sometime alienated and enemies in your mind by wicked works, yet now hath he reconciled.

O. Acts 24:16 and herein do I exercise myself, to have always a conscience void of offense toward God, and toward men.

P. Romans 8:1 there is therefore now no condemnation to them which are in Christ Jesus, who walk not after the flesh, but after the spirit.

Same Blame Game

Lesson 9
Ephesians 4:31-32
Stop **BLAMING** and forgive those who have hurt us

A. Write Ephesians 4:31-32 (Please read aloud)

_____
_____
_____
_____
_____
_____
_____

Definition of **BLAME:**
To find fault with; to hold responsible; to place responsibility for

Definition of **RESPONSIBLE:**
Liable to be called on to answer to; account as the primary cause

Let's take a look at blaming that took place in the Bible by the first two people on the face of our planet. READ Genesis 3:1-13
B. Write down Genesis 3:12

_____
_____
_____

C. Adam blames two individuals. Who were they? _____

D. What three words did Adam use for excusing his act of disobedience? _____

E. Write down Genesis 3:13

_____
_____
_____

F. Who does Eve blame? _____

G. What 4 words describe who she put the BLAME on?
_____

Blaming started in the Garden of Eden and has continued on throughout the centuries. No one likes to admit they might have had something to do with certain outcomes that came about because of our own choices. Guilt eats at us and instead of asking God and others to forgive us we look for someone else to blame. Of course there is another reason we blame and that is because it really is another person's choice that led to the situation we find ourselves in. Many of us, including the author of this program, have blamed in both scenarios. Many of us, including myself, have been very emotionally, physically, and spiritually wounded by not only our own unhealthy choices but by another person's choice as well. Adam and Eve realized they had made a very bad choice by not obeying Gods' instruction and they immediately hid themselves. They felt guilt and shame just as we have. Adam and Eve did as we have all done, they didn't **acknowledge**, instead they did wrong and blamed.

H. Have you ever felt like life would be different if it hadn't been for another person's wrong, sin choices?
_____

I. Have you ever blamed your parents, relatives, strangers, spouse, boyfriend or girlfriend, boss, etc., for your present circumstances? _____

J. Have you ever said, "If you only knew what happened to me, you'd know why I blame?" _____

K. Has blaming affected your past or present lifestyle? _____

L. Write down who you have blamed in the past and why.
_____
_____
_____

M. Write down whom you are blaming right now and why.

_____

_____

Now that we have taken inventory of just who we have blamed in the past or present, we need to see if there is any personal accountability that we should own up to, so we can be healed emotionally. The reason I know is because I personally let the enemy of my soul get me stuck emotionally on this step lesson. This blame game mentality brought about much needless misery to my life that I became very hardhearted, bitter and vengeful. As we let the Holy Spirit search our hearts and minds, he will show us if there was any wrong choice we may have done.

Some of our circumstances had absolutely nothing to do with our own choices and in actuality was another person's fault. The problem is that we tend to get stuck for days, weeks, or years and waste precious time that God has given us. We can't live in the past and hold onto old wounds. It eats us alive with anger, bitterness and resentment. It truly is time to give God all our cares.

N. Write down I Peter 5:7 (Please read aloud)

_____

_____

Our choices do affect others. Let's look in the Bible and see how Adam and Eve's choices affected their own family. Read all of Genesis Chapter 4. Adam and Eve's disobedience brought sin into the world that would affect not only their family but also families of all the people who would ever live since that time. As you have read, the first two children would reap what their parents had sown. Can you imagine the day they buried their son whose own brother had killed him? I never heard a sermon on this but I'm sure they were blaming each other for this great sorrow. I believe that all of us at one point in time of our lives have blamed someone, maybe even God for our grief. God extended mercy and forgiveness to them even though consequences follow disobedience.

Adam and Eve evidently accepted God's forgiveness and forgave one another as well as themselves or else in Genesis Chapter 5 they wouldn't have had more children. If they had been like most of us, they would have left each other and spent the rest of their days alone, without God and each other. They might have messed up with their first request from God but they made a U-turn and listened to God when He told them to be fruitful and multiply.

Our continued blaming will get us stuck. Our only way out is accepting forgiveness from God of our own wrongdoing. Then we must forgive ourselves and forgive all those who you have blamed, whether you feel they deserve it or not. We don't really deserve to be forgiven for our sins, but Jesus extended that to all when he died on the cross.

O. Read and write Luke 23:34

_____

_____

_____

If Jesus can forgive his tormentors, can't we also? More importantly, he expects us to forgive. It's a requirement for our own salvation and forgiveness.

P. Forgiving others is not an option. Read and write out Matthew 6:14-15

_____

_____

_____

_____

Why not let God heal your broken heart and relieve you of the deep, deep pain you've experienced for so long? Those that have hurt you won't get away with evil as it may seem. God sees all, knows all and there is a judgment coming.

Q. Read and write down Romans 12:19

_____
_____
_____

R. Write down Ephesians 4:32 again

_____
_____
_____

We don't want his vengeance on us for anything, so let's make our peace with God and others now and have that peace and serenity that will follow as a result.

Just say a simple prayer like this:
Jesus, if you could forgive all those people who tortured and murdered you, please help me to find forgiveness for all those that have hurt me and my loved ones. I ask you to take all this bitterness, anger and resentment away from me. I accept your love and forgiveness and I want to extend the same to them. Thank you for sending me this message so I could find peace and serenity and start the healing process of recovery. **Amen**

At this very moment if you truly meant that prayer, God has forgiven you. Continue to let Him heal your broken heart as you extend forgiveness to others and most of all, yourself.

RECOVERY TODAY
& EVERYDAY!

Reference Section for Same blame Game

A. Ephesians 4:31-32 Let all bitterness, and wrath, and anger, and clamor, and evil speaking, be put away from you, with all malice; and be ye kind one to another, tenderhearted, forgiving one another, even as God for Christ's sake hath forgiven you.

B. Genesis 3:12 And the man said, the woman whom Thou gavest to be with me, she gave me of the tree, and I did eat.

C. Eve and God

D. She gave me

E. Genesis 3:13 And the Lord God said unto the woman, what is this that thou hast done? And the woman said, the serpent beguiled me, and I did eat.

F. Serpent

G. The serpent beguiled me.

N. I Peter 5:7 Casting all your care upon Him; for he careth for you.

O. Luke 23:34 Then Jesus said, Father, forgive them; for they know not what they do. And they parted his raiment, and cast lots.

P. Matthew 6:14-15 For if ye forgive men their trespasses, your Heavenly Father will also forgive you; But if ye forgive not men their trespasses, neither will your Father forgive your trespasses.

Q. Romans 12:19 Dearly beloved, avenge not yourselves, but rather give place unto wrath; for it is written, I will repay, saith the Lord.

R. Ephesians 4:32 And be ye kind one to another, tenderhearted, forgiving one another, even as God for Christ's sake hath forgiven you.

(L.U.I.) Living Under the Influence

Lesson 10
Lamentations 3:40
DAILY examine our self and ask God's forgiveness

A. Write down Lamentations 3:40 (Please read aloud)
_____
_____

Lesson 10 needs insight
Definition of **INSIGHT:**
The power or act of seeing into a situation; the act or result of apprehending the inner nature of things; discernment, understanding, comprehension

Definition of **DISCERNMENT:**
To distinguish between; to detect with senses other than vision; to come to know or recognize mentally

Discernment stresses accuracy as in reading character or motives in both self and others. Through the power of the Holy Spirit in us, he points out to us what we need to have or not have in our lives.

B. Write down verses Psalm 139:23-24
_____
_____
_____
_____

Let's take an honest look into our hearts right now concerning our actions, attitudes, and motives, inner character.
Definition of **SEARCH:**
To look into or over carefully or thoroughly in an effort to find or discern something; to examine in seeking something; to uncover; to find or come to know by inquiry or scrutiny

Definition of **TRY**:
Examine; to put to test or trial; to test the power of endurance; prove, purify, refine

C. Let us allow the Holy Spirit to take his searchlight into our hearts and inspect us as to our character flaws or sin that may be there. Sometimes we don't even recognize that some garbage has crept in until God points it out to us, through the inner voice of the Holy Spirit. He can also show us these things through His Word, hearing a sermon, a friend, or in any way he chooses. We all need a good inner house cleaning. It's called the process of sanctification that we must do all throughout our lives. Be honest and willing and you will be blessed.

Write down some things the Holy Spirit is telling you right now.
_____
_____
_____
_____
_____

INSIGHT is a deeper understanding that is needed to examine our hearts to not only find those sins, but also show us why we feel or do those things that are not pleasing to God. Things that ultimately bring consequences that can cause us not only harm, but also those that our life influences. There is always a root cause of our actions and attitudes.

D. Write down Job 32:8 (Please read aloud)
_____
_____
_____

God will give you understanding if you ask him.
E. Write down James 1:5 (Please read aloud)
_____
_____
_____
_____

Let me ask you some questions. I've had to do this myself in the past and will have to continue this process until I go be with the Lord.

- Are our attitudes and actions influenced by people, places and things?
- Do our present and past circumstances, including our childhood, influence us?
- How about our environment? Past and present
- Does what we see, hear and read influence our character? TV, music, books, movies

All these things mold our character. There are positive, Godly influences and there are negative, ungodly influences. When we become born again and receive the Holy Spirit, He gives us insight. He shows us what and who needs to be removed from our lives so we can live a Godly lifestyle.

F. Write down some names of people who have had a negative, ungodly influence upon you, past or present.

_____
_____
_____

G. Write down some names of people who have had a positive, Godly influence on your past and present.

_____
_____
_____

How about your life? Have you always been a good influence upon others lives? Before I became a Christian, I didn't even realize how important my behavior really was upon others lives, especially my children. I figured I wasn't hurting anyone else but in reality my actions and attitudes affected everyone. Even now as a Christian I know I'm not in any intentional sin but my goal is to every day ask the Lord to show me any bad character issues that crop up. I ask him for help to remove them, so I can be a better Christian witness and ultimately please my Lord and Savior, Jesus Christ.

Definition of **INFLUENCE:**
To affect or alter by indirect or intangible means; to have an effect on the condition or development of

Definition of **MODIFY:**
To make a basic or important change

Definition of **SWAY:**
To cause to turn aside; to exert a guiding or controlling influence upon

H. Write down some names of people who were once influenced by your ungodly behavior such as children, spouse, family, parents, siblings, employer, and employees.

_____
_____
_____
_____
_____

At one time, I think many of us have said, "What I'm doing isn't hurting anyone", when in reality it did. Our actions and attitudes cause a ripple effect, positive or negative, to either help or hurt others. I for one no longer want to hurt anyone else and I desire to please my Savior, Jesus Christ.

A few years before I became born again, I signed myself into a government run addiction treatment center as a client, twice. Later, after surrendering my life to Jesus, I worked in one. I trained as a counselor for a while then became an outreach worker and later was promoted to Intake Coordinator. Between both these experiences, I now realize certain principles from the Bible were used in these programs. One of their suggestions to stay clean is to get away from people, places and things that would influence you to go back to your old lifestyle. Let's look at some scriptures that could have derived from that idea.

I. Read 2 Corinthians 6:14-18 and write verse 17

_____
_____
_____
_____

J. Write down Psalms 1:1   (Please read aloud)

_____
_____
_____

K. Read all of Proverbs Chapter 1 and then write verse 10

_____
_____

L. Write down Proverbs 1:15 (Please read aloud)

_____
_____
_____

M. What is God telling us in these verses about certain people who are a bad influence for us?

_____
_____

God is directing us to not be enticed, influenced, to not consent, go along with their way of thinking or acting, and to not walk, go along with what they're doing.

N. Read Proverbs 1:22-32 and write down verse 31

_____
_____

O. Write down Proverbs 1:33 (Please read aloud)

_____

P. Write down 2 Thessalonians 3:6-7 (Please read aloud)

Q. What is God telling us in these verses?

When I was a brand new Christian, no one had to tell me that I shouldn't hang with my old friends that used alcohol or drugs. The Holy Spirit inside me told me. I knew I would be influenced to go back to my old lifestyle if I did. I also immediately knew to beware of the music I listened to as well. The words and beat stirred in me the desire for my old life. I also used to watch soap operas and various other ungodly movies and shows on TV and I instantly realized how evil the content was. I had been addicted to pornography and when I surrendered my life to Jesus that night it vanished. I instantly hated what I once craved. I realized how important it was to be careful what I placed before my eyes and ears. When you make a whole heart commitment to Jesus, a supernatural miracle happens. God opens your Spiritual eyes to not only detect evil but now hate it as much as God does. These are just some examples of the ungodly influences that we can be aware of if we truly desire to live a Godly lifestyle.

Prior to the Holy Spirit living in me, I struggled with discipline. Saying no to destructive issues was virtually impossible in my own strength and will power. I could go only so long, days, weeks, even months and then I'd be right back to the same pattern. Praise God after committing my life to Jesus, the Holy Spirit in me has now made the power to say no finally possible. I can now discipline myself to be careful who I associate with, what I watch, what I listen to and what I read.

R. Read Luke 9:23-25 and write down verse 23

_____
_____
_____

S. Do you see how that verse relates to your life? Are there people, places, and things that have been a harmful negative influence upon you? To continue living a life pleasing to God write down what needs to be avoided to prevent you from returning to your old lifestyle. *This is your relapse/backslid prevention plan.*_____

_____
_____
_____
_____
_____

T. Write down Isaiah 41:10 (Please read aloud)

_____
_____
_____

Remember you can overcome any sin or addiction not by your power and strength, but by his! In conclusion, if you want to live under His influence, you can do so by examining your actions and attitudes and then simply ask for his forgiveness and power.

Say this prayer aloud:

Heavenly Father, I want to thank you for loving me and sending your son, Jesus Christ to die for my sins. Thank you for forgiving my sins. As I read your Holy Scriptures, and listen to the Holy Spirit's voice inside me, I desire to live under your influence. I want to not only please you but also be a good influence as a witness to others. I love you!   **Amen**

If you stumble and fall along your life's journey, don't stay in that rut. Reach out to God and let him restore you. Don't get the mentality though that you can continue in intentional sin and everything will be fine. That's a scary place to be. As you realize His great love for you, you'll want to please Him. That's who and what motivates me to keep living under the influence of the Holy Spirit, not people, places & things.

**Recovery is Possible
Today & Everyday!**

Reference Section for
L.U.I. Living Under the Influence

A. Lamentations 3:40 Let us search and try our ways, and turn again to the Lord.

B. Psalm 139:23-24 Search me, O God, and know my heart: try me, and know my thoughts: And see if there be any wicked way in me, and lead me in the way everlasting.

D. Job 32:8 But there is a Spirit in man: and the inspiration of the almighty giveth them understanding

E. James 1:5 But if any of you lack wisdom, let him ask of God, that giveth to all men liberally, and upbraideth not; and it shall be given him.

I. 2 Corinthians 6:17-18 Wherefore come out from among them, and be ye separate, saith the Lord, and touch not the unclean thing; and I will receive you, and will be a Father unto you, and ye shall be my sons and daughters, saith the Lord Almighty.

J. Psalm 1:1 Blessed is the man that walketh not in the counsel of the ungodly, nor standeth in the way of sinners, nor sitteth in the seat of the scornful.

K. Proverbs 1:10 My son if sinners entice thee consent thou not

L. Proverbs 1:15 My son; walk not thou in the way with them; refrain thy foot from their path.

N. Proverbs 1:31 Therefore they shall eat of the fruit of their own way, and be filled with their own devices.

O. Proverbs 1:33 But whoso hearkeneth unto me shall dwell safely, and shall be quiet from fear of evil

P. 2 Thessalonians 3:6-7 Now we command you, brethren, in the name of our Lord Jesus Christ, that ye withdraw yourselves from every brother that walketh disorderly, and not after the tradition which he received of us. For yourselves know how ye ought to follow us; for we behaved not disorderly among you

R. Luke 9:23 And he said to them all, If any man will come after me, let him deny himself, and take up his cross daily, and follow me

T. Isa. 41:10 Fear thou not; for I am with thee; be not dismayed; for I am thou God: I will strengthen thee; yea I will uphold thee with the right hand of my righteousness

Intimacy with My Shepherd

Lesson 11
Colossians 1:9-10
Have a **PERSONAL Relationship** with him, seeking his will

A. Write down Colossians 1:9-10 (Please read aloud)

_____
_____
_____
_____
_____
_____

B. Do you have a desire to know his will for your life?____ Do you want to live a lifestyle that pleases God?____ Do you want to be fruitful, successful in what you're doing to introduce others to Jesus, the Good Shepherd?____ Do you want to increase your knowledge of who God is? _____

If you answered yes, this lesson will help you be better able to do that. Using God's Word, the Holy Scriptures, we will lay a foundation to build on as to how you can know God's will for your life and have the ability to do it. First of all, if you have not made a decision to surrender your life to Jesus Christ, you won't be able to do this. You will need the Holy Spirit in your life who is not only our guide and teacher but reveals who Jesus is. This is what the Bible refers to as being born again.

Instantly, upon being born again, you belong to him and become one of his beloved sheep. He becomes your God, your Heavenly Father, your Good Shepherd. Right after I got saved I looked up to the sky and called him, Daddy God. I knew I belonged to him! My earthly father did not treat me as a good father should, so this thought was awesome. I didn't know it until later that the proclamation I made was actually in the Bible.

C. Write down Romans 8:15-16   (Please read aloud)

_____
_____
_____
_____
_____

The Hebrew word Abba means Daddy! We become adopted into his family, as one of his children. We become part of his flock, one of his sheep! In verse 16 since God is a Spirit, his Spirit speaks to our Spirit, telling us we now belong to him. This is why Christianity is not a certain denomination or religion but actually a **personal relationship** with God, through Jesus Christ.

D. Write down John 14:6   (Please read aloud)

_____
_____
_____

E. Write down Psalm 100:3   (Please read aloud)

_____
_____
_____

F. Write down I Corinthians 6:19-20 (Please read aloud)

_____
_____
_____
_____

As you can see from these verses our bodies, our lives do not really belong to us, but to God. He redeemed. bought us at a great price, his very own life. His blood shed on Calvary gave us the ability to be forgiven of sin and addiction of any kind. He also broke the Devil's power over us, enabling us to not only obtain but also maintain a Godly lifestyle. Of course it's our choice whether we want him to take his rightful ownership over us or not. Prior to being saved we've lived our lives as if we had the right and ownership over ourselves. We lived our life by what we wanted to do, following our own way of handling life's problems and stresses. There is a spiritual battle for our soul and we have let ourselves be under the evil shepherd's ownership without even realizing it.

Now that we have read scriptures showing us we belong to the Good Shepherd, let's look at some verses that prove he actually knows us by name. We are also going to look at scriptures that tell us that he hears us, he sees us and desires to help us with any situation we're in. He knows each of us personally and desires an intimate relationship with us!

READ John 10:1-1 Jesus calls himself the Good Shepherd and refers to us as sheep. Read aloud verses 3-5 this chapter proves he knows us personally. Now it's up to us to get to know him personally. Remember Col. 1:10 our scripture that goes along with lesson 11 says, May we increase our knowledge of God. That is the purpose of this study. As we realize who he is and who we are in him and that he desires to walk and talk with us, it should make us want to respond back to his voice of love calling us.

G. Write down John 10:14 then read aloud

_____

_____

We are going to read some scriptures that will help you to be God conscious, Shepherd conscious, aware of his presence.

H. Write down Hebrews 13:5   (Please read aloud)

_____

_____

_____

I. Write down Psalm 23:4   (Please read aloud)

_____

_____

J. Write down Psalm 91:15 (Please read aloud)

K. Write down Joshua 1:9 (Please read aloud)

L. Write down Deuteronomy 31:6 (Please read aloud)

Now we're going to read scriptures that tell us his eyes see us and his ears hear us.

M. Write down Job 34:21 (Please read aloud)

N. Write down Psalm 34:15 (Please read aloud)

O. Write down Psalm 34:4 (Please read aloud)

P. Write down Psalm 18:6 (Please read aloud)

Q. Write down I Peter 3:12 (Please read aloud)

_____
_____
_____
_____

Prayer is not repetitious words that we repeat over and over. You wouldn't have a conversation with your loved one or friend in that manner. God is a Spirit, we can't see him but we know from the scriptures he is always with us, hears us, and talks to us. He created us to have companionship with him. In the book of Genesis when God created Adam and Eve, He walked and talked with them in the garden. Disobedience ruined that since God is Holy. God through Jesus Christ restored that broken relationship. Let's look at some synonyms for the words intimate and relationship.

Synonym for **INTIMATE:**
Close, dear, cherished, warm, near

The antonym, opposite of intimate is *DISTANT*

Synonym for **RELATIONSHIP:**
Bond, rapport, connection, link, association

When you walk and talk with God, pray and read his Word, the Holy Spirit in you will reveal God's will for your life. You will also find the power and strength as you pray and read the Holy Scriptures.

R. Write down Psalm 138:3

_____
_____
_____

After learning the wonderful truth about your Good Shepherd, wouldn't you like to get to know him better and have an intimate relationship with Him? You can! The choice is yours. Spend time talking and listening to Him, read his Word, go to church, hang out with other Christians, be a doer of the Word, not just a hearer of the Word (James 1:22). If that is your desire let's pray.

Pray this simple prayer:
Dear Jesus, I'm so glad you are *my* Good Shepherd and I am y*our* sheep. *I belong to you!* I'm glad you're always with me, hear me and see me. I want to get to know you better and I realize this will take time from my daily schedule. You are number one in my life and I will go to any lengths to have a close intimate relationship with you. You sacrificed your very own life to make *me your own* and the least I can do is return my love to you!

I am yours! You are mine! I belong to you!

RECOVERY TODAY & EVERYDAY! MY SHEPHERD'S WAY!

Reference Section for Intimacy with My Shepherd

A. Colossians 1:9-10 For this cause we also, since the day we heard it, do not cease to pray for you, and to desire that ye might be filled with the knowledge of his will in all Spiritual understanding; that ye might walk worthy of the Lord unto all pleasing, being fruitful in every good work, and increasing in the knowledge of God.

C. Romans15:16 For ye have not received the spirit of bondage again to fear; but ye have received the Spirit of adoption, whereby we cry, Abba, Father. The Spirit itself beareth witness with our spirit, that we are the children of God.

D. John 14:6 Jesus saith unto him, I am the Way, the Truth, and the Life: no man cometh unto the Father, but by me.

E. Psalm 100:3 Know ye that the Lord he is God: it is he that hath made us, and not we ourselves; we are his people, and the sheep of his pasture.

F. I Corinthians 6:19-20 What? Know ye not that your body is the temple of the Holy Ghost which is in you, which ye have of God, and ye are not your own? For ye have been bought with a price: therefore glorify God in your body, and in your Spirit, which are God's.

G. John 10:14 I am the Good Shepherd, and know my sheep, and am known of mine.

H. Hebrews 13:5 Let your conversation be without covetousness; and be content with such things as ye have; for He hath said, I will never leave thee, nor forsake thee.

I. Psalm 23:4 Yea, thou I walk through the valley of the shadow of death, I will fear no evil; for thou art with me; thy rod and thy staff they comfort me.

J. Psalm 91:15 He shall call upon me, and I will answer him; I will be with him in trouble; I will deliver him, and honor him.

K. Joshua 1:9 Have I not commanded thee? Be strong and of a good courage; be not afraid; neither be thou dismayed; for the Lord thy God is with thee withersoever thou goest.

L. Deuteronomy 31:6 Be strong and of a good courage, fear not, nor be afraid of them: for the Lord thy God, he it is that doth go with thee; He will not fail thee, nor forsake thee."
M. Job 34:21 For his eyes are upon the ways of man, and he seeth all his goings.
N. Psalm 34:15 The eyes of the Lord are upon the righteous, and his ears are open unto their cry.
O. Psalm 34:4 I sought the Lord, and he heard me, and delivered me from all my fears.
P. Psalm 18:6 In my distress I called upon the Lord, and cried unto my God: He heard my voice out of His temple, and my cry came before him, even unto his ears.
Q. I Peter 3:1 For the eyes of the Lord are over the righteous, and his ears are open unto their prayers; but the face of the Lord is against them that do evil.
R. Psalm 138:3 In the day that I cried thou answeredst me, and strengthenedst me with strength in my soul.

Purpose- Help Others Recover

Lesson 12
Matthew 28:19-20
Living a Godly lifestyle, we **HELP OTHERS RECOVER!**

A. Write down Matthew 28:19-20   (Please read aloud)

_____
_____
_____
_____
_____
_____
_____

Those verses are referred to as the **GREAT COMMISSION.**

Definition of **COMMISSION:**
A formal written warrant granting the power to perform various acts or duties; an authorization or command to act in a prescribed manner or to perform prescribed acts; authority to act for, in behalf of, or in place of another; a group of persons directed to perform some duty

Our formal written warrant giving us this command is the Bible, God's written Word. The one who gives this command and gives us the power to act is our commander and chief, Jesus Christ.

This command that Jesus gave his disciples was right after he had resurrected. This command has to include you and I and not just his disciples or this awesome truth would have ended when they all eventually died. So in order for the continuance of this beautiful love story, all generations to follow had to be commissioned as messengers so others could learn the truth and become part of his family. I for one am glad that people throughout the ages have been bold to the point of risking or even losing their lives for this cause. All of us who are saved are a result of people following the great commission.

B. Write down John 17:18 (Please read aloud)

_____
_____
_____

C. Write down John 17:20 (Please read aloud)

_____
_____
_____

D. What were the last three words of that verse?

_____

There's a great story about a *woman evangelist* in the book of John chapter 4. I'm going to give some very important facts about the history and culture of that era as to better help understand this beautiful story. During that time, Jews were very prejudiced against the Samaritans, as some Jews had intermarried. They despised them so much they went out of their way so as not to pass through their town. Men also treated women as lower class. Jesus said he needed to go through Samaria. Nothing is coincidence in life or just lucky. Jesus went there knowing this woman would be there as it was about noontime. During that time of day, it was the hottest and people generally went to the wells in the morning or evening. At that time of day the likelihood of anyone being there with a bucket would be slim. In verse 11 she tells him he has no bucket to draw water with, so he had to have come for the very *purpose of revealing who he was to her*, not because he was thirsty. This proves also that Jesus is not prejudiced against any race or culture of people. He also considered this woman, even with her immoral lifestyle very valuable to the Kingdom of God.

A common practice during this time was that when you went to draw water, you brought your own bucket, as there was none left there and the wells were deep. Many Bible scholars who have studied the culture of that era have said that the reason this woman came at the hottest time was because she was an outcast to her neighbors because of her lifestyle. She carried a lot of shame and guilt and probably was tired of the whispers and gossip about her. Getting water was a social event for the day. It was very common in those days for men to divorce their wives for any little thing, not just adultery. A woman couldn't divorce the man. There were many divorces then, as there is now, because we are all looking for someone to fulfill our lives. Jesus knew this woman had suffered rejection and longed for true love and acceptance. I believe this is why he had such love and compassion for her as he had seen her broken heart, guilt and shame. We were created to find total fulfillment in a love relationship with Him as our bridegroom and us as his bride.

E. Jesus pointed out to her what her sins were in verse 18. Although He knew her sins, He came to show her he loved her anyway. She *acknowledged* he had spoken the truth about her. What did Jesus know about you the day he revealed himself to you? Were you feeling guilt and shame? Were you looking for love and fulfillment in all the wrong locations and faces? Maybe you didn't have a lifestyle like this woman but yet you felt empty, thirsty and did other things to find fulfillment. Write down your thoughts relating your life to this story.

_____
_____
_____
_____
_____
_____

In verses 21-24, they're discussing where to worship and how. We get in those debates when talking about denominations and the various rituals that differing churches have. Jesus shares with her in verses 23-24 that it's not most important where or how but whom you worship

In the prior chapter, Jesus tells us that we must be born again. When Jesus started telling this woman of the living water, he's referring to *receiving* the Holy Spirit.

F. Write down John 4:13-14

_____
_____
_____
_____
_____
_____

Due to scarcity, water was of special value in Palestine. There was heavy rain in the fall and light rain in the spring. During the rest of the year, the springs would dry up. Water supply was limited to those who had good wells. A common practice was man made cisterns that would catch rainwater. Getting a drink from a deep well like Jacobs' well was supposed to be a real treat as it was very cold, quenching the thirst.

G. Write down Jeremiah 2:13
_____
_____
_____
_____

Without Christ in our life we look to manmade ways to satisfy our thirsty souls. Nothing satisfies like the Holy Spirit inside us. In verse 13, Jesus tells her that she would never be satisfied with natural water. In verse 14, He refers to the water he gives will be spiritual, bringing not only everlasting life but bringing a life with contentment, satisfying her deepest longing to love and be loved. I'm sure she understood this analogy because of the abusive relationships she'd endured.

In verse 26, Jesus reveals himself to her! In verse 28, she left her water pot, symbolic of leaving her old lifestyle behind.

H. If Jesus has revealed himself to you, write down how He has fulfilled your thirsty soul.
_____
_____
_____

If you notice in verses 28-42 she immediately went back to the town *evangelizing, fulfilling the great commission* She had met the love of her life. She had found what she had been looking for all her life. She now had a *lifestyle with purpose*. God was going to use her to **help others recover!**

In verse 29, I can almost hear the excitement in her voice at the realization of this intimate meeting. She truly had the living water bubbling up within. She now had the love and compassion of God within her, wanting others to know him. I'm sure she'd been rejected and ridiculed by many of these people, yet she wanted others to have this living water, the Messiah, Jesus Christ!

I. In verse 39, write down in your own words what happened.

_____

J. In verses 41-42, write down in your own words what happened.

_____
_____
_____

Here's an awesome thought: Jesus could have easily gone into the city himself and revealed himself to the whole crowd. He didn't because he wanted to show you and I how he much he cares about each one of us personally. He knows all about us - the good and bad - and that doesn't keep him from loving us. He has seen that in our pursuit of happiness our lives have become so broken by drinking from man-made wells. We do that by trying to satisfy our lives through relationships, material things, career, homes, etc. God gives us all these things to enjoy but what we were created for is an intimate loving relationship with him, making him our first love and priority.

K. Write down John 4:35

_____
_____
_____

Jesus may have been pointing to the huge crowd that came out to see for themselves who he was when he made that statement to his disciples. This verse should stir our hearts to do as this woman did. She realized her town needed him just as much as she did. They might not have lived a lifestyle like she did but we know God's Word says, all have sinned. We also know every human being on this earth is not truly satisfied, content, and fulfilled if they don't have a personal relationship with our Savior, Jesus Christ.

L. Write down 2 Peter 3:9

The Lord is telling us that he's not willing for any to perish but that all should come to repentance. If that is your heart's desire too, then **say this prayer aloud**:

Jesus, I'm so glad you came to me and revealed my need for you. Now Lord, use me in this end time harvest. Use me to reach all those who are brokenhearted and looking for something or someone to make them truly happy. Thank you for loving me enough to not only die so I could be forgiven, but for your great love and mercy. Thank you for letting me be part of the great commission by giving me a:

Lifestyle with Purpose!

I want to help others recover!
Today & Everyday!

Reference Section for
Purpose-Help Others Recover

A. Matthew 28:19-20 Go ye therefore, and teach all nations, baptizing them in the name of the Father, and of the Son, and of the Holy Ghost; teaching them to observe all things whatsoever I have commanded you: and, lo, I am with you always, even unto the end of the world.
B. John 17:18 As thou hast sent me into the world, even so have I also sent them into the world.
C. John 17:20 Neither Pray I for these alone, but for them also which shall believe on me through their word
D. Through Their Word
F. John 4:13-14 Jesus answered and said unto her, Whosoever drinketh of this water shall thirst again: But whosoever drinketh of the water that I give him shall never thirst; but the water that I give him shall be in him a well of water springing up into everlasting life.
G. Jeremiah 2:13 For my people have committed two evils; they have forsaken me the fountain of living waters, and hewed them out cisterns, broken cisterns, that can hold no water.
I. They believed on him for the saying of the woman which testified
J. Many believed by her words. Others sought him out for their selves and after He spoke to them personally, many more believed.
K. John 4:35 Say ye not, there are yet four months, and then cometh harvest? Behold I say unto you, lift up your eyes, and look on the fields; for they are white already to harvest.
L. 2 Peter 3:9 The Lord is not slack concerning his promise, as some men count slackness; but is longsuffering to us, not willing that any should perish, but that all should come to repentance.

www.ingramcontent.com/pod-product-compliance
Lightning Source LLC
Chambersburg PA
CBHW060815050426
42449CB00008B/1663